POLITICAL PERCEPTIONS OF THE PALESTINIANS ON THE WEST BANK AND THE GAZA STRIP

ANN MOSELY LESCH

Special Study Number Three

THE MIDDLE EAST INSTITUTE

Washington, D.C.

CONTENTS

Document:

Maps:

PREFACE

The West Bank and the Gaza Strip were occupied by Israel in June 1967. The West Bank had been annexed to Jordan in 1949 and the Gaza Strip had been ruled by Egypt since 1948. The two areas comprise about a quarter of the historical territory of Palestine and are inhabited at present by approximately 1.2 million Palestinian Arabs. More than 400,000 live in the Gaza Strip and some 800,000 on the West Bank, including 105,000 residents of East Jerusalem. These Palestinians form a third of the Palestinian people; another half a million reside inside Israel and more than 1.5 million live in exile in Jordan, Syria, Lebanon and other countries.

The Palestine Liberation Organization (PLO), founded in 1964 by the Arab League and banned in the territories held by Israel, has become the militant voice of the Palestinian people and is widely recognized as their diplomatic spokesman. This study does not analyze the policies of the PLO but rather focuses on the political attitudes of the Palestinians inside the occupied territories. It attempts to present Palestinian aspirations today and the ways in which their views have evolved over the thirteen years of Israeli rule.

I would like to express my appreciation to the Middle East Institute for its support for my study. Dr. Emile A. Nakhleh, Philip Mattar, and Dr. Richard Erb provided welcome encouragement and useful advice. Muhammad Muslih and Maha Abu Dayyeh helped me translate some of the Arabic materials.

The people to whom I am most indebted live on the West Bank and the Gaza Strip. Ever since I first visited the occupied territories in September 1968, I have learned from the many Palestinians who have shown me unlimited kindness and have given me insight into their experiences and aspirations. While I worked in Jerusalem from 1974 to 1977 as associate representative of the American Friends Service Committee, and on my frequent visits since then, I came to know members of municipal councils, UNRWA employees, businessmen, clergy, professionals and intellectuals. I visited refugee camps and villages, and tried to understand the concerns of people from all parts of the society. I also benefited from discussions with many Israelis and foreigners working there as volunteers, journalists and consulate staff. I would be pleased to list the Palestinians here, but the continuing sensitivity of the subject compels me to refrain from naming them. I am sure that they know how much I appreciate their friendship as well as their help. It is also evident that I bear the sole responsibility for any errors of fact and misinterpretation that appear in this monograph.

Ann M. Lesch
March 20, 1980

Chapter 1

PALESTINIAN ASPIRATIONS AFTER CAMP DAVID

P alestinian residents of the West Bank and the Gaza Strip articulate a clear consensus concerning their political aspirations. They demand the end to Israeli military occupation and they seek self-determination for the Palestinian people. They assert their right to form an independent state which would establish through negotiations peaceful relationships with neighboring Israel and Jordan. These demands have been stated in numerous resolutions and petitions issued by the municipalities, professional societies and charitable groups on the West Bank and Gaza. For example, an unpublished petition that was signed by more than sixty civic leaders in June 1979 declared:[1]

> We aspire to establish a just and lasting peace in the region, which can only be on the basis of our people's exercising their right to self-determination and national independence, after the complete [Israeli] withdrawal from all the territories and the establishment of the independent Palestinian state.

That political position is fundamentally different from the bellicose propaganda of Ahmad Shuqayri, who was appointed by the Arab League to head the Palestine Liberation Organization in 1964. It also differs from the credo of the PLO that called for a democratic secular state in all the territory of historical Palestine. The process of change in

Palestinian thinking has been carefully charted by the political analyst Sabri Jiryis[2] and has been articulated by Yasir Arafat, the chairman of the Executive Committee of the PLO: "I offered a democratic secular state, but they said we wanted to demolish and destroy Israel. We put it aside and said we will establish our independent state in any part of Palestine."[3]

Palestinian leaders recognize the need for an interim period—preferably under international supervision—before full independence is achieved. A transition phase would not only reduce Palestinian and Israeli fears about each other's intentions, but would also minimize dislocations within the Palestinian community. Arafat told a U.S. Congressional delegation that he would welcome the "protection" of United Nations forces for a prolonged period.[4] And he later reiterated that "the only possible solution" is joint US-Soviet guarantees for Israel and the Palestinian state, adding:[5]

What do you think will endanger peace more—having the Palestinians as they are, deprived of their national rights, their human rights, scattered here and there, having ill treatment everywhere, or having the Palestinians settled as normal civilians with their national pride restored and with a flag of their own?

The institutions necessary for a state already exist. The Palestinian diaspora has the structure of the PLO—the Executive Committee, Palestine National Council (the parliament-in-exile), the Red Crescent Society and its clinics and hospitals, SAMED industries, schools in Lebanon and Kuwait, and affiliated women's, students' and workers' associations. Some of these could be transformed into governing and administrative bodies. Within the West Bank and the Gaza Strip there are municipalities and village councils, and a complex network of charitable and professional societies that provide medical, social welfare, educational and economic services.[6] Moreover, Palestinian staff presently serve under the Israeli military administration and are responsible for assisting the residents in the fields of agriculture, social services, health and education. And the United Nations Relief and Works Agency (UNRWA) has a substantial bureaucracy that has served the refugees since 1948. While some of the UNRWA institutions would need to be retained to care for those refugees, many of its Palestinian employees could contribute their administrative skills to the new state.

It is increasingly apparent that the Palestinians must represent their own interests in the negotiating process. No Arab state can speak authoritatively on their behalf. Only the PLO, as the recognized leadership of the Palestinians, can put the stamp of legitimacy on a diplomatic settlement and enable that settlement to be consolidated. Exclusion from the diplomatic process ensures that the Palestinian leadership will oppose the results of the negotiations and that the Palestinians will remain a destabilizing force in the region. Moreover, the Palestinians living in the territories occupied by Israel cannot—and do not want to—organize themselves to negotiate. They comprise only a third of all the Palestinians, and they feel that they have neither the authority nor the political strength to represent the Palestinians as a whole. One West Bank resident commented wryly: "As things are [the mayors] have to apply to the [Israeli] military governor for spare parts for their municipal vehicles. How can they negotiate peace?"[7] Another remarked:[8]

Why don't the Israelis understand that it is very difficult for the people of the territories to undertake such a task? During World War II, when France was conquered by the Germans, Marshall Pétain did negotiate with Hitler. How was Pétain defined by his own people, if not as a

traitor? So also we define such people who organize themselves on the conquered territories in order to negotiate
with the conquering authorities.

Palestinian reactions to the Camp David negotiations and
the Egyptian-Israeli treaty must be set in the context of
their publicly stated willingness to accept a state alongside
Israel, their bitterness at being excluded from negotiations,
and their deep suspicion of Israeli intentions in the West
Bank and Gaza. They have a profound fear that the accords
will perpetuate the occupation, rather than end it, and will
even lead to the annexation of the West Bank and Gaza by
Israel. This fear is based on statements by Prime Minister
Menachem Begin, government actions such as the seizure of
land for Israeli settlements, and Palestinians' pervasive belief that the United States government will never persuade
the Israeli régime to relinquish the territories.

The Autonomy Proposals

The Israeli government announced a "self-rule" plan for
the territories in December 1977, which subsequently
served as the basis for the initial Israeli negotiating position
on autonomy. The self-rule plan proposed a five-year transition period in which a council would be elected on the West
Bank and Gaza Strip (with its seat in Bethlehem) that would
administer, but not legislate, on such matters as education,
health and social welfare. The council would not have the
authority to limit Israeli land purchases or settlements, and
Israel would continue to control both internal and external
security. Residents would choose between Israeli and Jordanian citizenship, but would not create a Palestinian legal
identity. Although the question of sovereignty would remain open for review after five years, the proposal emphasized that "Israel stands by its right and its claim of sovereignty" to those territories.[9]

The Camp David agreement of September 1978 included both a treaty between Egypt and Israel (signed in March 1979) and a "framework" for a comprehensive peace. Although the treaty terms were clearly defined, the framework was ambiguous in content and conditional in its time frame. A "self-governing authority" would be elected to replace the Israeli military government. Israeli forces would be reduced and redeployed "into specified security locations," joint Israeli-Jordanian patrols and control posts would be established on the borders, and the authority would have "a strong local police force" at its disposal. Negotiations among Egypt, Israel, Jordan, and representatives of the Palestinian people would "define the powers and responsibilities of the self-governing authority." By the third year of the five-year transition period, negotiations would be conducted on the territories' final status. Palestinians displaced from the territories in 1967 could be readmitted with the concurrence of all the negotiating parties, but no provision was made for the return of refugees from the 1948 war. The framework represented an improvement over the Begin self-rule plan in that it limited Israel's military presence, placed the police under the Arab authority's control, and compelled the Israeli government to acknowledge both the applicability of UN Security Council Resolution 242 to the territories and "the legitimate rights of the Palestinian people." But the framework did not address the issue of Jerusalem, admit the unity of the Palestinian people, or mention land and settlements. Moreover, determination of political sovereignty was left until the end of the transition period. The framework also assumed that Jordan would play an active role in negotiating, implementing and policing the agreement.

Subsequent statements by the American and Egyptian governments emphasized the aspects of the framework that seemed favorable to the Palestinians. Egyptian officials insisted that East Jerusalem was an integral part of the West

Bank, and therefore subject to the authority of the autonomy régime. They maintained that the Palestinian police would handle internal security, that the régime would have full legislative and judicial, as well as administrative powers, and that autonomy meant a period of preparation for self-determination and then independence.[10] Similarly, the US government emphasized that the Israeli military government should be abolished, that the basis of authority for the self-governing régime should be the negotiated agreement, and that residents of East Jerusalem should be able to participate in the autonomy régime. In one document President Carter asserted: "We regard the transition period as something essential for building trust . . . [so that] a final settlement . . . will fulfill the legitimate rights of the Palestinian nation on the one hand and [will] guarantee Israeli security and that of the other sides, on the other."[11] Moreover, the US government consistently viewed Israeli civilian settlements as illegal and criticized the establishment of new settlements as a stumbling block to negotiations.

The American and Egyptian positions implied that autonomy provided an opportunity for the Palestinians to break out of their political impasse and lay the base for an independent state. But many of the statements and actions by the Israeli government made autonomy seem a trap that would lead to the incorporation of the territories into "greater Israel." This was particularly apparent in the detailed recommendations submitted to the cabinet by the Ben Elissar interministerial committee, and similar documents presented by Justice Minister Chaim Landau, Agricultural Minister Ariel Sharon, and the three ministers from the National Religious Party. These documents stated that the military government would be withdrawn, but not abolished: therefore, the administrative council's source of authority would continue to be the military government. Israel would control all internal security, administer the Jewish settlements separately, enforce the right of Israelis to settle in the territories, and keep all state land and water resources under Israeli control. The Arab administrative council would not be allowed to legislate. Nor would it "be permitted to levy taxes, establish radio and TV stations, issue postage stamps and currency, control imports and exports, and hold elections according to lists and platforms."[12] The administrative council would not issue identity cards or passports, and its transport department would work under Israeli supervision. The education department would register students, train teachers and run museums and sports facilities but Israeli censorship would continue. The health department would be responsible for hospitals, clinics and related services, but a joint body would supervise such matters as inoculations.

The documents further specified that the Israeli army would control all traffic arteries, continue to use some 120,000 acres on the West Bank for training exercises, and have the right to arrest and search anyone anywhere in the territories. Prisons would remain under Israeli control, and the Israeli police would supervise the local police force. Jewish settlers would maintain their own police force and would be allowed to bear arms anywhere in the autonomous zone, not only within the settlements. Ariel Sharon declared: "Our troops will have the right to go into the casbah of Nablus ... and arrest people, search for weapons, and so on."[13] The military correspondent Zeev Schiff added that political subversion as well as military threats would have to be stamped out by Israel in the event, for example, that people in a village would form a PLO branch or the administrative council would print stamps with the name "Palestine" and pictures in memory of Deir Yassin.[14] Moreover, the majority of the cabinet asserted, shortly before autonomy negotiations began in May 1979, that Israel would never permit the establishment of a Palestinian state and that—after the five years of autonomy—Israel would claim sovereignty over all the territory.[15]

Some dissent was expressed within the cabinet against the terms offered for autonomy. The position paper presented by the Ministry of Defense, for example, argued that the negotiated treaty—rather than the military government—should be the source of authority for the Palestinian council, thereby implying that the council would acquire a legal identity independent of the Israeli system. Moreover, the Ministry's paper stated that the status of Jerusalem should be negotiable and that a joint—rather than solely Israeli—authority should be set up to control water resources and the allocation of water on the West Bank and Gaza.[16]

In late October 1979 Interior Minister Yosef Burg, who headed the Israeli negotiating team at the autonomy talks, agreed that the elections for the Palestinian council should be supervised by Israeli civilian personnel (rather than military officers) along with Palestinians from the territories, and that international electoral experts could observe all aspects of the process.[17] He also startled observers by suggesting that "should the PLO remove from its covenant all references to its aim to destroy Israel and replace it with a Palestinian state, and should it demonstrate for two or three years that it no longer engages in terrorist activities, this would no longer be the same PLO; and with one change triggering further changes, to my mind such a different PLO could make a suitable negotiating partner" for Israel.[18]

Nevertheless, the hardline statements were the ones backed up by concrete acts. In mid-December 1978 Israel ended a three-month freeze on settlement activity by expropriating 250 acres near Beit Sahour and fifty acres in Hebron. In the spring of 1979, 750 acres were seized north of Jerusalem near Neve Ya'akov settlement, and equivalent amounts of land were taken from the Ramallah municipality, and from Salfit and three nearby villages for the Ariel settlement.[19] The World Zionist Organization announced plans for 46 new settlements on the West Bank over the next five years, and the cabinet approved the establishment of several new *nahals* (paramilitary outposts) and civilian settlements during the summer and fall of 1979, including two in the Gaza Strip. The army sought to complete the expropriation of military sites before autonomy could come into effect, and militant settlers from Gush Emunim (Bloc of the Faithful) wanted to stake permanent claims on the West Bank. Moreover, construction began for a water pipeline from the Sea of Galilee south through the Jordan Valley in order to support a major expansion of settlements and consolidate Israeli control over water sources.[20] Four Gaza Strip settlements were organized into a regional council and the West Bank settlements were grouped into six regional councils in late 1979, thereby emphasizing their extraterritorial status and separation from the surrounding Arab communities.[21]

Some limitations were placed on the government's ability to establish settlements by the ruling of the High Court of Justice on the Elon Moreh case on October 22, 1979. In that unanimous decision, the justices rejected the security arguments presented by the Army Chief of Staff and maintained that the settlement served a political, rather than a security function, and thus could not be placed on private Arab land. The justices also underscored their argument in an earlier case that settlements should have a military security function, and thus remain only for the duration of the occupation and not remove the Arabs' ownership rights. Even though Elon Moreh had to be dismantled, the settlers simply moved to Jebel Kabir, another site near Nablus, and the government began to consider altering the legal status of the territories so as to bypass, in the future, any negative rulings by the High Court. Moreover, as a response to the murder of a Jewish student in Hebron on January 31, 1980, the government authorized Jewish settlement in the center of Hebron, initially in the form of two paramilitary religious schools.[22]

Opposition to government policy was highlighted by

Moshe Dayan's resignation as Foreign Minister in October 1979, the result of his objections to several government actions, including its approval of private land purchases by Israelis on the West Bank and Gaza, and its support for the establishment of Elon Moreh. He also criticized the government's failure to take unilateral steps that would persuade Palestinians that Israel intended "full" autonomy—rather than "token" self-rule—on the West Bank and Gaza. Such steps would have included allowing freedom of speech, press and assembly, and instituting a moratorium on settlements.

Some politicians outside the government were more outspoken in their criticism. One member of the Labor Party, for example, called the Ben Elissar proposals a "fraud" that meant continued Israeli military rule,[23] and an Israeli journalist asserted: "Even the most decided collaborator among the inhabitants of the territories will not agree to this format."[24] He added:

> If the intention is to establish an autonomy in the near future, does it make sense to forbid political organizing and political assemblies and to await the explosion of pent-up emotions? Is it wise to demolish houses and close off lands ... thereby angering the entire population just when we want to reach an understanding with them?

When the Minister of Defense arrested the mayor of Nablus, Bassam Shak'a, on November 11, 1979, and threatened him with deportation, the *Jerusalem Post* published a sharply worded editorial: "Truly, if an Arab city mayor ... cannot freely speak his mind even in private without being considered fit for punishment, then what is this thing called autonomy except a farce and a fraud?"[25] The international outcry over the mayor's arrest and the mass resignation of the mayors on the West Bank and Gaza helped to persuade the military governor of the West Bank to release Shak'a and reinstate him as mayor on December 5, 1979.

Other Israelis argued that autonomy would be an inherently unstable form of rule, which could lead only to annexation or independence. One columnist maintained that, in this case, "the self-governing authority will inevitably attempt to expand its powers until full sovereignty is achieved."[26] He described the Arabs' "acute desire for Israeli withdrawal and political independence,"[27] and another Israeli observer stressed the negative effects caused by Israel's tough actions against the Palestinians: "Almost every Israeli act in the territories strengthens the PLO. Each roadblock, each expulsion of inciters and each dispersal of a demonstration by the security forces build the identification and solidarity with the Palestinian nationality embodied in the PLO."[28]

Palestinian Reactions to the Autonomy Plan

Palestinian politicians on the West Bank and the Gaza Strip were stunned by the "framework" outlined at Camp David in September 1978. They had already expressed their firm opposition to the Begin self-rule plan, declaring that it legitimized Israeli control and made self-determination impossible. The mayor of Bethlehem had even declared that the Begin plan was "more humiliating" than the *status quo* since the administrative council would be "completely powerless—only figureheads without any real legislative or executive authority."[29] Those Arabs who backed the Israeli plan and accepted Israeli financial support were widely denounced on the West Bank. One senior politician in Hebron, Mustafa Doudin, was sharply criticized for accepting about I£500,000 from Israel for his "union of Hebron area villages," which the military government hoped would weaken the authority of the Hebron municipality.[30] In addition, the politician who was considered closest to the military authorities, 'Abd al-Nur Jenho of Ramallah, was assassinated in February 1978.

The Egypt-Israel agreement at Camp David caused dismay because it removed Egypt from the battlefield, thereby eliminating the most significant Arab pressure on Israel. Although the "framework" gave lipservice to Palestinian self-rule, residents feared that the self-governing authority would never be able to transform itself into a real government. Moreover, the framework gave Jordan a major role, which many Palestinians opposed, and made no provision for the two-thirds of the Palestinians who lived outside the occupied territories. The declaration issued by a hundred leading politicians on October 1, 1978, condemned autonomy as "legitimization of the occupation, the continuation of oppression of the [Palestinian] people and the stealing of their legitimate rights, and an open plot to curb the hopes of our people to have our right to our land and our self-determination."[31] Official Israeli interpretations of autonomy particularly distressed the Palestinians. One Arabic editorial listed Begin's "rigid" conditions:[32]

No—to the independent Palestinian state.
No—to the Palestine Liberation Organization.
No—to stopping Israeli settlements on the West Bank beyond three months.
No—to the withdrawal of Israeli troops from the occupied Arab lands.
No—to Arab sovereignty on the West Bank and the Gaza Strip.
No—to Arab sovereignty in Arab Jerusalem.
No—to a referendum of the Palestinian people.

A former Jordanian minister, Anwar Nusseibeh, commented to me that Camp David gave the "semblance of peace, but not real peace." After all, he said, the West Bank and Gaza are only the "rump" of Palestine and yet "we are denied even that rump." In other conversations in late September 1978, people stressed the flaws in the agreement: it split the Palestinian people and instituted an autonomy that seemed really a disguised occupation.

Several resolutions that were issued in September and October 1978 detailed the Palestinian arguments for rejecting the autonomy plan.[33] The essence of all these petitions was:

(1) The Palestinian Arabs are one people.
(2) The PLO is their sole legitimate representative.
(3) The self-rule plan legitimizes the Israeli occupation and prevents self-determination.
(4) A just and lasting peace can come only through the Palestinians' exercise of their right to self-determination and national independence, after complete Israeli withdrawal.
(5) Palestinian sovereignty must be established in East Jerusalem, which is an inseparable part of the West Bank.

From October 1 to November 7, 1978, the Israeli military government allowed the Palestinians to hold four public assemblies on the West Bank and two in Gaza. At the final rally 5,000 people assembled in Nablus on November 7.[34] These meetings unified opposition to the Camp David accords, stiffened resolve and boosted morale. After the Nablus rally, the military government reinstated the ban on political gatherings that had been rigorously enforced during the previous eleven years of occupation.[35] No further public meetings were allowed in any town. As a result, political expression moved underground: demonstrations began in mid-November and the number of bombings tripled from November to December 1978. On November 19, 1978, for example, the first anniversary of Sadat's visit to Jerusalem, two serious bombings occurred and students demonstrated in Ramallah.

عما لدول السعود وقراراتها . كما تسجل بالفخر المحاولات التنمية على طريق تلاحم العراق وسوريا .

الواقعية في صميم في سبيل عودتها الى دورها الرائد في النضال العربي .

كما وأيماننا بقيادة منظمة التحرير الفلسطينية الا مراكز الذي اكبر تعبيرا في مختلف اماكن تواجده وبمختلف العاصمة

من قيادة النضال الفلسطيني بجداره الى مستوى القضية الوطنية والقومية عربها ودوليا .

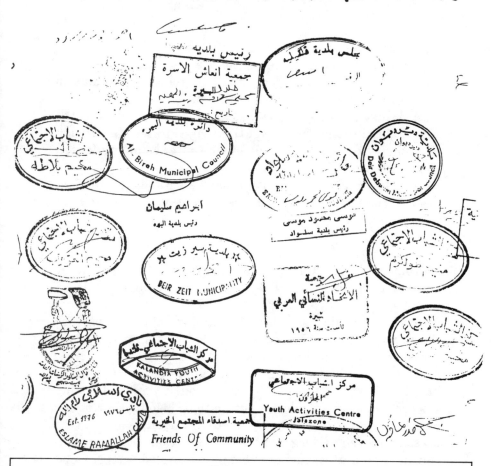

Document

Petition protesting Camp David that was circulated clandestinely in late September 1978, signed by more than 120 residents, including sixty members of village and town municipal councils. Excerpt shows the seals of the municipalities of Qalqilya, al-Bireh, Bir Zeit, Silwad, Deir Debwan, societies in six refugee camps, and other charitable groups.

Moreover, political views hardened and those who had backed Sadat's initiative fell silent. Although the elderly Shaykh Hashem Khuzundar of Gaza organized a group of residents to go to Cairo to support Sadat, the delegation's departure was delayed and many people dropped out of the delegation.[36] The mayor of Bethlehem commented that, if an autonomy council were imposed, "they could find some collaborators, but none of the mayors."[37] Those who met American envoys in late September and early October of 1978 stressed that they merely wanted to inform US officials clearly and directly about the Palestinian position, and would not appoint themselves as negotiators apart from the PLO.[38] Moreover, the statement that they delivered to US ambassador-at-large Alfred Atherton hardly differed from the public petitions.[39]

Although opposition to Camp David was expressed most vigorously by the active supporters of the PLO, the emergence of an overwhelming consensus against the accords was facilitated by the critical stand adopted by King Hussein of Jordan. At first, those West Bank residents who supported the King were uncertain of his position and kept relatively quiet. They tended to phrase their criticism in conditional terms. But the King soon authorized his supporters to participate in rallies and oppose the autonomy plan.[40] King Hussein felt humiliated by the role assigned to Jordan in Camp David and was angry that his participation had been taken for granted by the negotiators. Moreover, Jordan lacked Egypt's strength and room for maneuver, and therefore turned to tighter coordination with neighboring Saudi Arabia and Syria. As a result of the King's policy, the former speaker of the Jordan assembly, Hikmat al-Masri, addressed the mass rally in Nablus in November 1978 and the mayor of Gaza, Rashad Shawwa, who had close personal ties with the Jordanian monarchy, presided at a gathering in Gaza in mid-October 1978.

Moreover, King Hussein began a serious dialogue with the

PLO. A high level PLO delegation went to Amman in November 1978, and the King hosted Yasir Arafat in Jordan in March, August and December 1979. The initiation of the dialogue was supported by the PLO's Palestine National Council in a stormy session in Damascus in January 1979, and was strengthened by the establishment of a joint PLO-Jordanian committee to channel funds to the municipalities and societies on the West Bank and Gaza. One Arabic newspaper in Jerusalem welcomed the Palestinian-Jordanian rapprochement with the statement that effective coördination would be essential in order for the people in the territories to withstand the pressures to which they would be subjected over the coming months.[41] But there was widespread concern that the Arab states which opposed Camp David seemed unable to create an alternative diplomatic route, and that tensions between Syria and Iraq would weaken the Arab posture.

The public on the West Bank was shocked by the terms of the Camp David accord and agitated by Israeli actions. The demolition of a house by the Israeli army in December 1978 triggered a large demonstration in Ramallah the next day. After land was seized in Beit Sahour and Hebron that month, demonstrations spread through Bethlehem, Beit Sahour, Hebron and Halhul, and the Supreme Muslim Council and municipalities issued angry protests.[42]

In early January 1979, settlers in Kiryat Arba (near Hebron) demanded the use of the Tomb of Jacob in the main mosque in Hebron on Saturdays, even though the tomb was a Muslim holy place. Hundreds of settlers entered the tomb on Saturday, shoved aside Muslim worshippers and clashed with Israeli soldiers. The military government prevented the Arab mayor of Hebron from holding any public meetings to protest the settlers' behavior and the land expropriations, and in mid–January the government gave in to the settlers' demands that Jews use the tomb for part of the day on Saturday.[43] January 1979 also witnessed further bombings, and four more houses were demolished by the army. Once again there were demonstrations and commercial strikes in nearby towns.

The Egypt-Israel Treaty

The treaty negotiations between Egypt and Israel also prompted protests. Students stayed out of school during Carter's visit to Israel in mid-March 1979, and the final breakthrough in the negotiations was greeted by an outpouring of angry emotions. All the major towns and several villages were swept up in the protests, which included a massive general strike on March 26, 1979, the day the treaty was signed in Washington, D.C. The West Bank municipalities and a wide range of public figures in the Gaza Strip issued strong denunciations of the treaty. The West Bank statement criticized the "hostile intentions" of the US and Egypt as well as Israel, and asserted that the US was conspiring with Israel to legalize the occupation.[44] The Gaza declaration called the treaty signing a "painful occasion" because it "directly harms our legitimate rights and national aspirations." The manifesto reaffirmed their commitment to the PLO, "which is the symbol of the [Palestinians'] unity and the expression of their will in all forums" and maintained that the Palestinians would not relinquish their legitimate rights.[45] The Arabic press also reflected the belief that the US lacked political credibility. Al-Quds, the largest circulation newspaper, commented that the US gives promises, but takes no initiative or responsibility to guarantee that it will persuade Israel to withdraw and will enable Palestinians to establish their independent entity:[46]

The United States has not come up with any proposals that reflect its concern about solving the Jerusalem issue, its appreciation of the sensitivity of this problem and Arab and Muslim rights in the city. The US has not even satisfied its moderate friends (such as Jordan and Saudi Arabia). It has entered into confrontation with them without trying to understand their position. This has led to increasing fears and suspicion over the ambiguity of the US position.

The keen disappointment in Sadat was also evident. Whereas in November 1977 many believed that he would demand a comprehensive settlement, and even in September 1978 some hoped that he would link the treaty to negotiations on the West Bank and Gaza, he had now signed a separate treaty. He had regained Sinai for Egypt, but left the Palestinians stranded. Even conservative politicians such as Anwar Khatib, the former governor of Jerusalem, stated publicly that autonomy could not provide the minimum needed by the Palestinians: "The people of Palestine want peace, but not at any cost . . . [Anyone who] heads a government under the occupation, he will be another Abu Raghal [Quisling] of Islamic history."[47] And the former minister Anwar Nusseibeh remarked that Israel would be glad to rid itself of "small administrative details" in the occupation, but that would not be a real change. "Reassure me about my land. How can we be sure that it won't be worse after five years? Their settlement program goes on, their ideology, their power."[48]

During the spring the military government reacted harshly to manifestations of opposition. Halhul endured a fifteen-day curfew in March 1979 after Israeli settlers shot to death two youngsters during a demonstration.[49] Similar but shorter curfews were clamped on several refugee camps in April and May. Soldiers also broke into schools in Ramallah and Bir Zeit in March, and settlers from Ofra rampaged through Ramallah on March 13.[50] Clashes occurred in al-Haram al-Sharif in Jerusalem, when Jewish militants tried to pray at the Muslim holy place. And merchants protested by closing their shops in Jerusalem on March 24.[51] Israeli independence day (May 2, 1979) was marked by a huge Gush Emunim march on the West Bank, which Arabs attempted to counter by school strikes and an unauthorized procession of ten mayors inside Nablus. The mayors protested both the Israeli march and the extensive land expropriations. On that day, a settler from Neve Tzuf wounded a student from Bir-Zeit University. Instead of punishing the settler, the military government closed the university until July.[52] It was only reopened after intense public and private pressure from Israeli and foreign academic figures, and diplomatic representations by the US government. Other educational institutions were also closed by the military authorities, including Bethlehem University (for four days in May) and, in late March, two women's teachers training institutes and the boys' secondary school in Ramallah.

The mayors deplored the arrests and fines levied against the students. Fahd Qawasmah, the mayor of Hebron, asked how the Israelis thought people would act now that public gatherings were banned:[53]

What do they expect? That we should be submissive and obedient and not protest against such brutal offences? If we protest and demonstrate, they put us in prison, and if we remain silent, they confiscate our lands. And then you want us to show understanding and consideration.

Qawasmah added later: "The Israelis think that if only the mayors would shut up, the West Bank Palestinians would cooperate. They couldn't be more mistaken. What people on the streets in my town are saying makes me look like a moderate."[54] And the arrest of Bassam Shak'a, the mayor of Nablus, for three weeks in November 1979 deeply angered the West Bank residents, triggering the resignation of the

Nablus municipal council and a general strike in the city. All the other mayors resigned *en masse* when the Israeli government threatened to deport Shak'a, and the action compelled residents of every political persuasion to label the autonomy plan a cruel joke.[55]

Even though the united efforts of the West Bank and Gaza politicians helped to induce the Israeli military governor to release Shak'a and reinstate him as mayor of Nablus on December 5, 1979, there were few other victories for the Palestinians that winter. The threat to take over the East Jerusalem Electricity Company, the expropriation of additional semi-urban land near Hebron and East Jerusalem, and the formalization of Israeli-Egyptian relations with the exchange of ambassadors on February 26, 1980, all represented further setbacks to the Palestinians. The informal Committee for National Guidance, which comprised leading residents of the West Bank and Gaza, introduced an important element of cohesion. The Committee organized student and commercial strikes in response to those actions, banned contact with the Egyptian embassy in Tel Aviv, and tried to convene rallies in Jerusalem. But the military government banned the mayors from attending a Palestinian national assembly scheduled for al-Aqsa mosque in Jerusalem on February 19, 1980. Hebron endured a lengthy curfew after a Jewish student was shot to death there on January 31, 1980, and also faced the prospect of the introducing of militant Israeli settlers into the heart of the city.[56]

Minimal Conditions for a Transition Period

Palestinian politicians have been anxious that their criticism of autonomy not be interpreted as opposition to negotiations of any sort or to a genuine peace settlement. Mayor Karim Khalaf, of Ramallah, declared "We say 'yes', 'yes' to a Palestinian state and 'yes' to a just peace."[57] And Mayor Rashad Shawwa of Gaza commented reflectively: "I would appeal to the people of Israel to recognize the legitimate

rights of the Palestinians, accept the idea of self-determination for the Palestinian people and their right to erect their
own sovereign state. If this is done, if the problem of the
land is left to the autonomy authority, if settlement is
stopped and existing ones are dismantled, there are good
chances of coexistence."[58]

One issue that has caused considerable concern is the possibility of a "Gaza first" solution. This means that autonomy
would first be negotiated for the Gaza Strip, separately from
the West Bank. Sadat suggested that option during the winter of 1978–79 because he believed that he wielded more influence in the Strip than on the West Bank. He also felt that
autonomy in Gaza could serve as a model for autonomy on
the West Bank. But the Israeli government seemed to be
only interested in the Gaza option if it meant splitting Gaza
from the West Bank. Mayor Shawwa may have tried to test
the idea during his trip to Amman and Beirut in November
1978. Moreover, the Khan Yunis mayor, who visited Cairo in
February 1979, stated that he would accept self-rule in Gaza
first, "but only if we know that it will be linked to the West
Bank and eventually lead to full self-rule."[59] Shawwa re-
ferred to the pressures that both Israel and Egypt could
bring to bear on Gaza residents if they wanted to force a
settlement on them. Israel could deny residents access to
jobs in Israel, shut off electricity, and block shipments of
produce to Jordan. Egypt could expel the 10,000 Gaza students from its universities and reactivate its pre-1967 network of employees. But Sadat seemed to drop the idea of
"Gaza first" in the spring of 1979.[60] The only figure who
openly embraced the concept, Shaykh Hashem Khuzundar,
was assassinated on June 1, apparently by a Popular Front
fida'i, a turn to violence that was widely condemned in Gaza
and disowned by the PLO.[61]

Still, many residents grasped at straws. When the Israeli
Foreign Minister Moshe Dayan said in February 1979 that
Israel could not ignore the PLO and must settle the refugee

problem, some Palestinians saw a glimmer of hope. The mayor of Bethlehem called Dayan's remarks a step in the right direction and a newspaper editor added that, if Israel recognized the PLO, there would be a chance for a peaceful solution and for the two nations to live together in peace.[62] Although Dayan "clarified" his comment the next day— saying he did not mean that Israel should negotiate with the PLO, but that one could not ignore the PLO's influence in the region—some people on the West Bank still tried to find hints of a policy change in his statement. One editorial remarked that Dayan was not a political novice, given to slips of the tongue, and that this might be the beginning of a realistic trend in Israeli policy, forced on it by events in the Middle East.[63] Later, when Dayan resigned from the government, his move was widely interpreted as a sign of the bankruptcy of the autonomy policy.[64]

Similarly, when opposition leader Shimon Peres spoke in the Knesset about Palestinian national rights, two of the Arabic newspapers immediately noted that his speech contained positive elements. The conservative newspaper, *al-Quds*, for example, commented that although Peres rejected the idea of an independent Palestinian state and a return to the 1967 borders, his "remarks contained more than one new and important position.... What was implied in his speech is that it is impossible to ignore the Palestinians' right to set up a homeland."[65]

In conversation, members of municipal councils and other civic leaders say that they realize that an interim period is required before they can become an independent state alongside Israel. Some list conditions that must be met before the negotiations can be taken seriously, such as a freeze on settlements during the interim period; an Israeli commitment to eventual withdrawal of its armed forces; a statement of the Palestinians' right to self-determination; efforts to reach an equitable accord on Jerusalem, and provision for gradually implementing the refugees' right to return.[66]

Fahd Qawasmah stated: "If Israel says this is the land of the Palestinians, then we can discuss security, future relations between us, how to arrive at peace, a hundred items. But the aim of the negotiations must be clear from the start."[67] In May 1979 Qawasmah added that he and the other mayors would persuade the PLO to join the negotiations *if* Israel would state that it would evacuate settlements, withdraw from all the territories, grant the right of self-determination to the Palestinians, and return Jerusalem to its pre-June War status.[68] The mayors of Gaza and Bethlehem made similar statements, arguing that if they could gain these preconditions, they would try to persuade the PLO to support negotiations.[69]

I have attempted to extract from discussions with Palestinians, as well as from their statements for the public record, minimum conditions that they feel they need if a transition régime is to win acceptance. No one person has listed all these conditions; rather, they form a composite picture drawn from many conversations over an extended period. Meeting these conditions during negotiations—or during the interim period itself—would ensure that the régime would not be a step toward annexation by Israel, but rather a step toward independence alongside Israel.

The ruling council on the West Bank and Gaza would require secure financial resources, including the power to levy direct and indirect taxes, and to receive loans and grants from abroad. The council would have authority over the administrative departments (social welfare, education, health, agriculture, industry and commerce, tourism, customs, postal service and police), and would have clearly delineated responsibilities *vis-à-vis* the municipalities and village councils. The council would administer the land registry department and public land as well as property that Israel designated "absentee" land because its owners were abroad in 1967. The council would also regulate the use of water and mineral resources. Since Israeli settlements are located on public, absentee and private lands, and tap local water sources, the council would be able to prevent any increase in the number or size of settlements and, ultimately, could negotiate their removal. (If Israelis seek to live in the West Bank or Gaza without claiming extraterritorial status, special arrangements could be negotiated.)

The passage of people and goods between the West Bank and Gaza Strip (presumably on a specified road across Israel) and across the Jordan bridges would be guaranteed in the negotiations. The council would be able to develop Gaza as an international transit port, and would use the Kalandia airport, north of Jerusalem. The special security measures required at border checkpoints would be detailed in the negotiations.

The right of refugees from the wars of 1948 and 1967 to move to the West Bank and Gaza would need to be established during the negotiations, although their return would have to be phased carefully as part of a comprehensive program of economic development. Identity cards would be provided for returning refugees as well as for current residents, but the issue of providing Palestinian passports for those Palestinians who would remain abroad could probably be deferred until a later stage in the negotiations.

If Israeli armed forces were limited to specific points along the Jordan River and to observation posts on the central mountain ridge, and if internal security were in the hands of the Palestinian police force, then the Palestinians could tolerate an Israeli presence during the transition phase. Israeli patrols would not be allowed to roam the city streets, enter houses at will, and arrest residents. The military court system would be dismantled, and the Palestinian council would control the judiciary and prisons. Palestinians would welcome the presence of UN or other neutral forces in the West Bank and Gaza to protect the legitimate security needs of both the Israelis and Palestinians.

The issue of Jerusalem would be central to the negotiations. Even setting aside its importance as a religious center to Muslims, Christians and Jews, East Jerusalem serves as the commercial, educational and political headquarters of the West Bank chambers of commerce, trade unions, and professional and charitable societies. Jerusalem has the greatest concentration of hotels, tourist agencies, shops, insurance companies and banks, and serves as the central market for fresh produce and meat. The Supreme Court (closed down in 1967) is located there, along with the pre-1967 offices of the government and municipality. At a minimum, its 105,000 Arab residents need the right to vote for and participate in the governing council of an interim régime. But in order to assure the long term viability of an accord, East Jerusalem would need to become the capital of the Palestinian state. The city would remain open physically, but many Palestinians would prefer that it would be administered by separate Israeli and Arab municipalities, with a joint coordinating committee for certain services.

It is evident that all these conditions cannot be met before an interim régime is established. Indeed, many of them will have to be worked out through the process of negotiations. But Palestinian mistrust of American and Israeli intentions is so intense that more than "verbal clarifications"[70] will be required at the initial stages. Linkage of implementation of the Israel-Egypt treaty to an agreement on the West Bank and the Gaza Strip, and inclusion of the PLO in the negotiations would be tangible steps. Similarly, a freeze on Israeli settlements, a commitment to place government lands under the authority of the Palestinian council, and a timetable for withdrawing Israeli military rule would be practical measures that would indicate the ultimate outcome of the transition period.[71] Most of all, the concept of reciprocity and mutual respect needs to be introduced into Israeli-Palestinian relations. Those concepts were at the heart of the Israel-Egypt accord but have been denied to the Palestinians and Israelis.

NOTES, CHAPTER 1

1. Original in Arabic.
2. Sabri Jiryis, "On Political Settlement in the Middle East: The Palestinian Dimension," *Journal of Palestine Studies*, number 25, autumn 1977, pp. 3–25.
3. Transcript, "Face the Nation," CBS TV, December 3, 1978. See also "News from Congressman Paul Findley," December 1, 1978, which recorded his discussion with Yasir Arafat on November 25, 1978.
4. Unpublished transcript of Arafat's discussion with Findley and other members of a congressional delegation, Damascus, January 5, 1978.
5. Quoted by Anthony Lewis, *The New York Times*, May 4, 1978.
6. Emile A. Nakhleh, *The West Bank and Gaza: Toward the Making of a Palestinian State*, Washington, D.C.: American Enterprise Institute for Public Policy Research, 1979.
7. Quoted in *Events*, December 16, 1977.
8. The former Jordanian minister Anwar Nusseibeh, quoted in *Davar*, December 20, 1977.
9. *The Jerusalem Post* international edition, January 3, 1978.
10. Sadat letter to Carter, September 17, 1978; Cairo, Middle East News Agency and radio broadcasts, May 10, 1979; *al-Ahram* (Cairo), February 5, 1980, printed the text of the Egyptian autonomy plan.
11. *Ma'ariv*, April 17, 1979, reported Carter's response to King Hussein in October 1978.
12. *Ha'Aretz*, May 21, 1979. See also *Ha'Aretz*, January 8, 1979, *Jerusalem Post*, February 11, 1979, and *The New York Times*, February 10, 1979.
13. *The Christian Science Monitor*, May 9, 1979.
14. *Ha'Aretz*, January 16, 1979.
15. *Ha'Aretz*, May 22, 1979; *The New York Times*, May 22, 1979. Those basic positions did not alter during the autonomy talks: see Israeli radio broadcasts of December 28, 1979, and January 3, 1980, *Ha'Aretz*, January 14, 1980, and the critique by Mark Heller, "Israel's False Autonomy," *Foreign Policy*, number 37 (Winter 1979-80), pp. 111–132.
16. *Ma'ariv*, May 9, 1979.
17. *The New York Times*, October 27, 1979, and *The Christian Science Monitor*, November 8, 1979.
18. Quoted in *Jerusalem Post* international edition, November 4–10, 1979.
19. Reuter, November 28, 1978, reported the 46-settlement plan; *The New York Times*, November 15, 1978, reported the Gaza Strip buffer; *Jerusalem Post*, November 1 and 9, 1878, reported the "fleshing out" of colonies; new *nahals* were announced on Israel TV, January 14, 1979; con-

fiscation near Neve Ya'akov was reported on the Israeli radio January 31 and February 2, 1979; withholding land from Ramallah municipal use was noted in *Yediot Ahronot*, February 1, 1979; the land expropriation for Ariel was reported on Israel radio April 18 and 17, 1979; cabinet approval of two settlements was covered in *Ma'ariv*, April 23, 1979 and *The New York Times*, April 24, 1979; and the construction of Elon Moreh was reported in *The New York Times*, June 4 and 8, 1979.

20. *Jerusalem Post* international edition, February 18–24, 1979, *Yediot Ahronot*, February 23, 1979.
21. Israel radio broadcasts, March 26, 1979, and January 2 and 28, 1980.
22. *Jerusalem Post* editorials, June 21 and October 23, 1979; *The New York Times*, October 23, 1979; *The Christian Science Monitor*, October 26, 1979 and February 21, 1980; Israel radio broadcast, January 31, 1980; Amnon Rubinstein in *Ha'Aretz* and Daniel Bloch in *Davar*, February 13, 1980. On the legal issues, see Uzi Benziman, *Ha'Aretz*, February 15, 1980.
23. Yossi Sarid, Labor Party Member of Parliament, quoted in *Jerusalem Post* international edition, February 11–17, 1979.
24. Yehuda Litani, *Ha'Aretz*, December 7, 1978.
25. *Jerusalem Post* editorial, November 12, 1979.
26. Benny Morris, *Jerusalem Post* international edition, November 21, 1978.
27. *Ibid.*
28. Dani Rubinstein, *Davar*, March 16, 1979.
29. *The New York Times*, July 20, 1978; also statements in *al-Fajr*, December 30, 1977, by several mayors.
30. *Ma'ariv*, December 27, 1978; *Ha'Aretz*, December 31, 1978; *al-Tali'ah*, August 31, 1978.
31. Unpublished statement, translated from the Arabic original.
32. *Al-Fajr*, September 26, 1978.
33. Resolutions were issued by the Arab Graduates' Union, the Union of Professional Societies, students at the UNRWA men's teachers' training institute in Ramallah, and at the Bir Zeit and Najjah rallies. None of the resolutions was allowed to be published in the newspapers by the Israeli press censor.
34. *Ha'Aretz, Jerusalem Post* and *al-Fajr*, November 8, 1978; *al-Fajr*, November 15, 1978.
35. Article one of Military Proclamation 101 (August 27, 1967) prohibits assemblies of more than ten persons in which an address is delivered on an expressly or implicitly political topic. Article six bans convening or participating in any meeting for which the military governor has not granted a permit. A person can be jailed for up to ten years for attending such a meeting. The reinstating of the ban was reported in *Ma'ariv*, November 14, 1978; *al-Fajr*, November 15, 1978; *The Financial Times*, November 18, 1978; and *Ha'Aretz*, November 19 and 26, 1978.
36. Israel radio broadcasts, October 17 and 24, 1978.
37. Elias Freij, quoted in the *Washington Post*, September 27, 1978.
38. The nine who met with Alfred Atherton on September 29, 1978, were

Hikmat and Thafer al-Masri of Nablus, Aziz Shehadeh and Nafez Nazzal of Ramallah, Anwar Nusseibeh of Jerusalem, Elias Freij of Bethlehem and, from Gaza, the mayor's nephew Mansour Hashem Shawwa, Dr. Hatem Abu Ghazaleh, and Fayez Abu Rahmeh. Four of the same people met with Harold Saunders on October 20, 1978 (Hikmat al-Masri, Aziz Shehadeh, Elias Freij and Hatem Abu Ghazaleh), joined by Gaza mayor Rashad Shawwa, Najla Mansour of Gaza, *al-Quds* editor Mahmud Abu Zuluf, UNRWA area director Antranig Bakerjian, and a member of the Jerusalem chamber of commerce, Faiq 'Abd al-Nur. Saunders also met privately with Anwar Khatib and others.

39. Original in English; not published.
40. Israel radio broadcast, October 15, 1978; IDF radio, October 25, 1978.
41. *Al-Quds* editorial, May 10, 1979.
42. *The New York Times*, December 17, 1978; *The Christian Science Monitor*, December 21, 1978; *Ha'Aretz*, December 29, 1978.
43. *Davar*, December 31, 1978; Israel radio broadcasts, January 4, 10 and 11, 1979; *Ha'Aretz*, January 5, 1979; *Jerusalem Post* international edition January 7–13, 1979; *Jerusalem Post*, January 19 and 21, 1979.
44. Original in Arabic; quoted by the Voice of Palestine broadcast, March 27, 1979.
45. Original in Arabic; quoted by the Voice of Palestine broadcast, April 14, 1979.
46. *Al-Quds* editorial, April 23, 1979. See also the *Jerusalem Post* international edition, April 23–28, 1979.
47. *Al-Ra'y* (Amman), December 14, 1978.
48. Quoted by Anthony Lewis, *The New York Times*, April 23, 1979.
49. *Financial Times* and *The New York Times*, March 16, 1979.
50. Curfews in Beit Ur Tahta village (*Ha'Aretz* March 20, 1979), Aqabat Jabr camp and Yamun village (*Jerusalem Post*, April 11, 1979), and Jalazun camp (*The Washington Post*, May 20, 1979 and *Jerusalem Post* international edition, May 20–26, 1979). The Ofra settlers' actions in Ramallah were reported in the *Financial Times*, March 15 and 16, 1979, and the *Jerusalem Post* international edition, March 18–24, 1979.
51. Israel radio broadcast, March 24, 1979, and *Jerusalem Post* international edition, March 18–24, 1979.
52. Joseph Harsch, *The Christian Science Monitor*, May 11, 1979; *Jerusalem Post* international edition, May 6–12, 1979; *The Washington Star*, May 28, 1979; and *The New York Times*, May 27 and June 14, 1979.
53. Fahd Qawasmah, mayor of Hebron, *Ha'Aretz*, December 29, 1978.
54. *The New York Times*, March 27, 1979.
55. *Washington Post*, November 9, 1979; *The New York Times*, November 12, 1979; and *The Christian Science Monitor*, November 13, 1979.
56. Israel radio broadcasts, January 3 and February 26, 1980; Israel news agency ITIM bulletins, January 3, February 1, 18 and 26, 1980; *The Christian Science Monitor*, January 3, February 7 and 21, 1980; *Jerusalem Post*, February 25, 1980.
57. *Jerusalem Post*, October 17, 1978.

58. Interview with David Mandel, *Israel and Palestine* (Paris), April/May 1979, p. 11.
59. *Jerusalem Post* international edition, March 25–31, 1979.
60. Rashad Shawwa quoted in *al-Ra'y* (Amman), May 8, 1979. Sadat's views are noted in *The New York Times*, November 15, 1978, *The Christian Science Monitor*, March 16, 1979, and the *Economist*, March 24, 1979. Israel's viewpoint is reported in *Ma'ariv*, May 14, 1979.
61. *The New York Times*, June 3 and 4, 1979; *The Christian Science Monitor*, June 7, 1979. The possibility of Gaza-first settlement was revived in the fall of 1979, as reported in *The Christian Science Monitor*, November 5, 1979, and in the *Jerusalem Post*, January 11, 1980.
62. Israel radio broadcasts, February 13 and 24, 1979; the latter quoted Mahmud Ya'ish, editor of *al-Sha'b*.
63. *Yediot Ahronot* and *al-Quds*, February 14, 1979.
64. *Davar*, October 22, 1979.
65. *Al-Hamishmar*, March 14, 1979, quoted an editorial in *al-Quds*.
66. Specific proposals for an interim period have been published by a few Palestinians, notably Mohammad Abu Shilbaya, "An Alternative to Autonomy," *New Outlook*, September 1978, pp. 47–50; Tony Klug, "When Enemies Dare to Talk," *New Outlook*, October 1978, p. 22; Ibrahim Matar, "Economic Dimensions of the Self-Governing Authority for the West Bank and Gaza," unpublished mimeographed paper, February 1979.
67. Fahd Qawasmah, mayor of Hebron, *The Christian Science Monitor*, March 29, 1979.
68. Israel radio broadcast, May 7, 1979.
69. Elias Freij, Israel radio broadcast, October 28, 1978; Rashad Shawwa, *Financial Times*, November 30, 1978 and *Jerusalem Post* international edition, March 25–31, 1979.
70. Muhammad Hasan Milhem, mayor of Halhul, *Wall Street Journal*, October 12, 1978.
71. The independent journalist Raymonda Tawil proposed four such "constructive Israeli actions" that could help to break down hostility, in her statement to the *New Outlook* symposium in Washington, D.C., October 28, 1979.

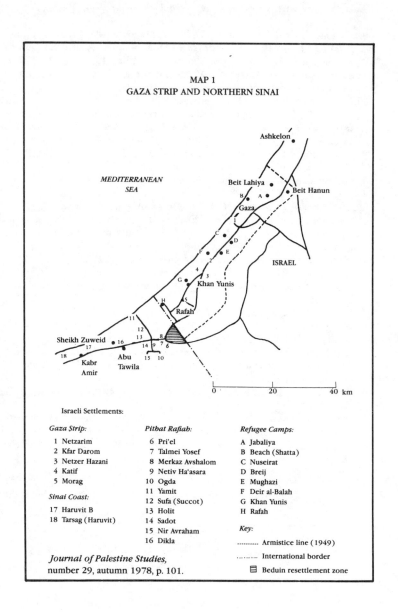

MAP 1
GAZA STRIP AND NORTHERN SINAI

MEDITERRANEAN
SEA

Ashkelon

Beit Lahiya

Beit Hanun

B   A

Gaza

ISRAEL

C

D

F   2   E

4   G   3

Khan Yunis

5

H

Rafah

11

12

13   8

Sheikh Zuweid   16

17   14   9   7   6

18   15   10

Kabr   Abu
Amir   Tawila

0   20   40 km

Israeli Settlements:

Gaza Strip:	Pithat Rafiah:	Refugee Camps:
1 Netzarim	6 Pri'el	A Jabaliya
2 Kfar Darom	7 Talmei Yosef	B Beach (Shatta)
3 Netzer Hazani	8 Merkaz Avshalom	C Nuseirat
4 Katif	9 Netiv Ha'asara	D Breij
5 Morag	10 Ogda	E Mughazi
	11 Yamit	F Deir al-Balah
Sinai Coast:	12 Sufa (Succot)	G Khan Yunis
17 Haruvit B	13 Holit	H Rafah
18 Tarsag (Haruvit)	14 Sadot	
	15 Nir Avraham	Key:
	16 Dikla	

.... Armistice line (1949)

.—..—.. International border

目 Beduin resettlement zone

Journal of Palestine Studies,
number 29, autumn 1978, p. 101.

30

Chapter 2

THE INITIAL YEARS OF OCCUPATION

At the time of the June War in 1967, a sense of national identity was reëmerging among the dispersed Palestinian people. But this nationalism could not be expressed effectively. The Palestine Liberation Organization (PLO), founded by the League of Arab States in 1964, had not developed an organizational structure at the grassroots level. The guerrilla organizations were still small and semi-clandestine. And the Arab régimes kept a tight rein on their Palestinian residents.

The war itself transformed the struggle. Israel gained control over the Sinai peninsula, the Golan Heights, the West Bank and Gaza. Israel thereby dominated all of pre-1948 Palestine and half of the Palestinian community: to the more than 400,000 Arabs inside Israel were added the million Arabs concentrated on the West Bank and the Gaza Strip. The other half remained in Lebanon, Syria and the East Bank of Jordan, with smaller numbers residing in Egypt, the Arab Gulf states, Europe and the Americas. The connection between the East and West Banks of the Jordan was severed: about 200,000 people fled from the West to the East Bank and the twenty-year process of "Jordanizing" the Palestinians ended abruptly for those who found themselves under Israeli control. The residents of the Gaza Strip lost their link with Egypt but reëstablished relations with the Palestinians on the West Bank, from whom they had been isolated since 1948. And both groups came into contact with the Arab citizens of Israel, providing the latter with their first exposure since 1948 to an intact, sophisticated Arab society, and leading slowly to the renewal of social (and political) bonds.

The immediate reaction to the occupation was shock, numbness and humiliation. Residents said that *Jabal al-Nar*, the "mountain of fire" that overlooks Nablus, was reduced to a "mountain of ashes" by the war. Many panicked and fled across the river, while others urged the residents to remain, fearing a repetition of the 1948 exodus. The economy was paralyzed, with banks closed, remittances blocked, and agriculture, building trades and tourism at a standstill. The situation was eased somewhat by the Israeli decision to allow agricultural produce to be shipped across the Jordan River to Amman. But otherwise economic life remained frozen. UN Relief and Works Agency (UNRWA) personnel provided emergency relief to people fleeing from the Latrun and Qalqilya areas, where the Israeli army demolished several villages and expelled their residents. UNRWA also assisted the municipalities which collected money from residents for distribution to the needy, acting in conjunction with the local Red Crescent societies, women's societies, and other charities.

Local committees were rapidly formed on the West Bank to organize political resistance against the occupation, under the loose coordination of several political activists. But three key leaders were deported in December 1967,[1] and the local committees in Jerusalem and Jenin were similarly smashed. Since Jordan had banned all political parties in 1957 and had only allowed the PLO office in Jerusalem to function for a year (1964–65), politicians had no means to organize political resistance.[2] The clandestine parties were weak and divided. The Arab National Movement (ANM), which followed the doctrines of George Habash, had fractured shortly before the war. Although its leaders reunited under the impact of the crisis, their advocacy of total non-coöperation and violence brought them into rapid confrontation with the Israelis. (They had much greater influence in the Gaza Strip, where the Nasirite ANM had been sanctioned by Egypt.) Ba'thist intellectuals had had wide popular support, but were demoralized by the defeat of Ba'thist Syria's army and the apparent failure of pan-Arabism to liberate Palestine. Only the Communist Party had an underground structure that enabled its cadres to continue their activities under occupation but, even so, many of its leaders were still held in Jordanian prisons and its actions were circumscribed. The strongest politicians were the pro-Hashimite notables and merchants who controlled the municipalities and religious institutions. They spoke out vigorously for a return to the *status quo ante,* and were therefore sharply opposed by the Israeli authorities. The president of the Islamic Court of Appeals, Shaykh 'Abd al-Hamid al-Sayih, was the first person deported by Israel, followed by the Jerusalem mayor, Rouhi Khatib, and several conservative doctors, judges and bank managers.

The Israeli decision to annex the Arab part of Jerusalem in June 1967 and to evict 200 Arab families from the Old City prompted the first public protests. Twenty Muslim leaders met at al-Aqsa mosque on July 24 and issued a manifesto denouncing the annexation. Israel immediately placed four of the participants under house arrest. The Arab municipal council in Jerusalem had already rejected Israel's proposal to join the amalgamated municipality, and protested to the United Nations on August 3.

Protests elsewhere on the West Bank were initiated by a memorial issued by 16 lawyers from Nablus in July and a mid-August declaration signed by a hundred West Bank residents that called for national unity and steadfastness against both the annexation of Jerusalem and Israeli attempts to form a separate "entity" on the West Bank.[3] The high point was marked by the National Charter of the Arabs of the West Bank for the Current Phase, issued by 129 prominent residents of Nablus, Jenin, Tulkarm, Ramallah, al-Bireh, Jerusalem, Bethlehem and Hebron on October 4, 1967.[4] Stating that the "Arab people of the West Bank are overwhelmed by calamity" in the face of "Zionist aggression," the charter asserted the need for collective Arab action on behalf of the Palestinian people, and affirmed that Jerusalem is an Arab city, holy to Muslims and Christians, and an integral part of the West Bank. It also supported the unity of the East and West Banks of the Jordan, but criticized the Jordanian government, maintaining that Jordan requires an independent, non-aligned foreign policy, and a democratic and constitutional régime. The Charter rejected both Judaizing and internationalizing Jerusalem, and inveighed against any proposals to establish a Palestinian state on the West Bank that would be linked with the "alien Zionist presence," denouncing such proposals as efforts to isolate the Palestinian people and remove the Palestine problem from its Arab context.

The National Charter represented a consensus among widely varying political tendencies: all who signed it assumed that the West Bank residents lacked the power to stand alone against Israel, believed that resistance must occur in the wider Arab context, and sought the return of the West Bank to some form of Jordanian rule. The idea of a separate state in only the occupied territories was viewed as a cover for Israeli control, rather than an assertion of Palestinian identity. The few who proposed such a state were sharply denounced, and their lives were even threatened.[5]

In addition to the manifestoes against the occupation, the associations of teachers and lawyers launched strikes during the fall of 1967. The lawyers' strike was occasioned by Israel's decision to move the Court of Appeals from Jerusalem to Ramallah. Terming the move illegal, most of the judges and lawyers refused to practice in the courts but continued to draw pay from the Jordanian government. The effectiveness of the strike was reduced when Israel authorized its own lawyers to practice in West Bank courts and, over time, many lawyers came to believe that they could serve the residents better by defending them than by boycotting the courts.

The school strike was more successful than the lawyers' strike, because it compelled the Israeli authorities to drop most of the changes they had planned to make in the curriculum.[6] In August 1967 the teachers had declared that there could be "no education under occupation"[7] but, as the occupation lengthened from weeks to months, a compromise was reached and most schools reopened in mid-November, under the banner of "no Judaization of education." By then, following the passage of UN Security Council Resolution 242 in early November, the politicians realized that the occupation would not end quickly and they would have to revise their strategy to prepare for an extended period of Israeli rule.

By mid-1968 the situation had begun to stabilize on the West Bank, with the economy slowly reviving and the municipalities and administrative units providing basic services for the residents. But sudden protests flared up on special anniversaries and in response to Israeli provocations. In the spring of 1968, strikes and demonstrations were held to protest the Israeli Independence Day parade in Jerusalem and to mark the first anniversary of the June War. On that day, the strike was almost totally effective in Nablus, Jenin, Tulkarm and Jerusalem, where a silent procession to the Muslim cemetery erupted into violence when Israeli police tried to block some of the marchers.[8] During the autumn of 1968, people protested in Nablus and Hebron against the demolition of houses, and in Ramallah they decried the intrusion of soldiers into several girls schools. (The mayor, Nadim Zaru, was detained for five days in October 1968,[9] and was deported the following year after leading protests against the army's demolition of a house.)

Tension was particularly high in Hebron after seventy Israelis settled in the town in April 1968 and demanded the right to pray at the Cave of Machpelah, located inside the Ibrahim mosque.[10] The mayor, Shaykh Muhammad 'Ali al-Ja'bari, chaired a meeting of municipal officials, members of parliament, professionals, members of the Chamber of Commerce, and workers in early May, which sent a delegation to the Israeli military governor protesting the presence of the settlers.[11] Ja'bari convened a meeting of 400 Hebron notables later that month and headed a delegation to Defense Minister Moshe Dayan on June 3, 1968. But the settlers were allowed to remain in Hebron, living initially in the military compound. They began to move into permanent housing in the newly constructed Kiryat Arba settlement in mid-1969, despite the continued protests by the Arab community.

Another general strike was held on the second anniversary of the June War. Immediately afterwards, nine strike leaders were deported to Jordan from Nablus, Tulkarm, Ramallah and Jerusalem. As troubles resumed in the schools during the fall of 1969, Israel deported more teachers, including the educational inspectors for Hebron and Nablus, and the principal of an UNRWA school near Ramallah. Dayan held the mayors and school principals responsible for maintaining order in the towns, rejecting the contention of the Nablus mayor that a strike was "a peaceful and legitimate action" and was "the only way to express the people's dissatisfaction with the present Israeli military occupation."[12] The authorities also quelled civil disobedience by closing shops, imposing travel restrictions, and fining and arresting demonstrators and shopowners. The military central command imposed a I£10,000 ($3,000) fine and/or two years' imprisonment on persons guilty of inciting others to strike or spreading propaganda hostile to the state of Israel; a I£1,000 ($300) fine and/or one years' jail against shopowners for closing their business on working days; and a

I£10,000 ($3,000) fine and/or five years' jail for closing shops during an organized strike.[13]

The actions of the residents on the West Bank were closely related to the wider Middle East context. The Arab states were stunned by their losses from the June War. Ahmad Shuqayri, appointed by the Arab League to head the PLO, was disgraced. Only the Palestinian guerrillas attempted to confront Israel. Guerrilla raids across the Jordan River harassed Israeli forces and raised Arab morale. The prestige of the *fida'iyin* soared after they inflicted losses on Israeli troops who raided their base in Karameh refugee camp, on the East Bank of the Jordan, in March 1968. The guerrilla organizations rapidly assumed control over the PLO, and Yasir Arafat, the leader of the largest group, Fatah, became the chairman. The PLO was transformed from a government-initiated propaganda body into an instrument of the fighting forces.

During 1968 and 1969 the rise of guerrilla activities was also marked by numerous bombings in Jerusalem and Israel of movie theaters, market places, and foreign consulates. But neither the internal unrest nor the guerrilla raids achieved any progress toward liberating the occupied territories. Moreover, international diplomatic efforts through the United Nations and the super powers produced no results, and both Egypt and Israel bled from the "war of attrition" along the Suez Canal in 1969–70. Civil and military resistance inside the territories resulted in large-scale arrests and deportations, and caused economic hardships, given the overwhelming power wielded by the Israeli military authorities. By mid-1970 one foreign correspondent reported:[14]

Those leaders who remain in the West Bank are paralysed ... Each town and village in the [West] Bank ... exists in an atomised isolation. Between a cunning provincialist like Shaykh Ja'bari of Hebron, a nationalist firebrand like

Mayor Masri of Nablus, and the Christian collaboration-ists of Bethlehem there is no scope for concerted action. Israelis and West Bank Arabs alike tend to keep their eyes glued to the Arab states and to the Great Powers.

Defense Minister Moshe Dayan had succeeded in his policy of atomizing the population and making the personal costs of resistance excessively high. He had also let the merchants and tourist business regain a high level of activity and allowed thousands of Arab laborers to work inside Israel, raising their cash income and buying temporary relief from political resistance. But only after the civil war in Jordan (September, 1970) did the prospects of military liberation seem to vanish. That shock jarred the residents into searching for new political strategies and more sophisticated political conceptions.

Political Currents After Black September

From June 1967 until 1970, the Arab states bordering Israel gave political and sometimes military support to the Palestinian guerrilla movement. Although the governments of Egypt and Jordan (but not Syria) adhered to UN Security Council Resolution 242, which acknowledged the existence of Israel and its right to secure borders, those régimes did not publicly criticize the demand by the PLO to replace Israel by a democratic secular state. But in mid-1970 the US-initiated Rogers' Plan offered Egypt and Jordan an opportunity to negotiate a settlement along the lines of UN Security Council Resolution 242. Regaining the lands lost in 1967 would thereby be accomplished at the price of recognizing Israel within its prewar limits. The guerrilla leaders of the PLO denounced the negotiations and set themselves on a collision course with these states, even though they relied on Jordan as a territorial sanctuary and on Egypt as a political and propaganda base. The *fida'iyin* had become a virtual state-within-a-state in Jordan, demonstrably undermining King Hussein's authority. The ensuing crisis in September 1970—sparked by the hijacking of planes by the most radical guerrilla group, George Habash's Popular Front—gave King Hussein his opportunity to unleash the Bedouin troops and eliminate the guerrilla presence on the East Bank.[15]

The fighting during "black September" destroyed West Bank residents' hope of liberation from the East, and devastated Jordanian-Palestinian relations. Palestinians on the West Bank sent numerous cables demanding that King Hussein abdicate. These were signed by leaders of trade unions, chambers of commerce, municipalities and professional bodies, representing a wide spectrum of political views. The former governor of Jerusalem and leading adherent of the King, Anwar Khatib, convened a meeting in his home to demand that the King resign.[16] The despair was reflected in the following comment:[17]

The people here, they feel now that whatever they do it's no use. We tried petitions, demonstrations, strikes—nothing worked. We tried grenades and sabotage—no use. We are punished and nothing changes. Now we just go about our business and hope something will happen and the Israelis will go away.

The supporters of the PLO and of the strategy of armed resistance were dismayed by the PLO's defeat in Jordan and the relatively ineffective regrouping the *fida'iyin* achieved in southern Lebanon. Israel's crushing of the guerrilla movement in the Gaza Strip by 1971 further demonstrated the inefficacy of isolated armed action. Nevertheless, PLO supporters held to the demand for a democratic secular state in all of Palestine, and adherents of leftwing groups such as the Popular Front and the Democratic Front redoubled their calls for social revolution in the Arab world as the prerequisite for the liberation of Palestine. In contrast, the Communists held to their position that all traces of Israel's 1967 aggression must be removed, which implied acquiescence to Israel's existence within the prewar lines and the realization of Palestinian rights on the basis of reunifying the East and West Banks.

Most of the established politicians on the West Bank called for a return to the *status quo ante*. Nablus dignitaries such as Hikmat al-Masri and Qadri Tuqan argued that Israeli evacuation must first be achieved, with the East and West Banks reunited, and then the Palestinians could settle their accounts with the King. In Jerusalem, a similar stand was adopted by the Muslim Council, the West Bank Chamber of Commerce, and elder statesmen such as Anwar Nusseibeh and Anwar Khatib.[18] A few of those notables argued that reunification must take place on a different basis than the prewar arrangement. For example, Hamdi Kan'an, the former mayor of Nablus, argued that Jordan must abolish personal rule and replace it by a national government that would reflect the public will: the king should work "now for amendment of the constitution to include an article granting the Palestinians self-government and linking them with the East Bank in a federation. . . . This would insure a genuine and equal unity."[19]

Only a small number of residents felt that the West Bank should establish a separate political identity even while it remained under Israeli military rule. Shaykh Ja'bari of Hebron, for example, sought district level administrative autonomy for the West Bank, a concept that was denounced as treasonous by all the other political factions.[20] He was not only accused of selling the Palestinians' heritage, but was especially charged with legitimizing the occupation and helping the Israelis to consolidate their hold.

Nevertheless, a trend began to emerge that supported the idea of a separate state on the West Bank and the Gaza Strip. Its adherents demanded that the occupation end and that a referendum be held under UN auspices so that the

Palestinians could exercise their right to self-determination and create an independent state. The leading daily newspaper in Jerusalem, *al-Quds*, argued that the Palestinians must stop waiting for the Arab leaders to fulfill empty pledges to liberate Palestine.[21] And some young teachers and intellectuals in Jerusalem held informal study and discussion groups during the winter of 1970–71 in which they formulated and weighed ideas, groping for a way to articulate their nationalist beliefs. The plan for a separate state was spelled out by the journalist Muhammad Abu Shilbaya in *No Peace without a Free Palestinian State*, in the fall of 1971. He proposed a five-year UN administration during which Palestinian refugees would return, IDs and passports would be issued, political parties organized, free elections held, and a national assembly convened that would elect a provisional government for the independent republic of Palestine.[22] The book caused a furor on the West Bank, although Abu Shilbaya himself was—and remained—marginal politically. Given the widespread animosity toward Jordan, the idea of a separate Palestinian state attracted considerable interest. However, most political figures believed that West Bank residents alone lacked the power to end Israeli rule and achieve independence, and so they feared that the outcome would differ little from the "autonomy" supported by Shaykh Ja'bari. Therefore Abu Shilbaya was criticized as politically naïve and defeatist. His articulation of this concept of statehood was still premature and heretical, but the study at least began to air the idea of establishing a state located in that part of Palestine which retained a substantial Arab majority.[23]

The Gaza Strip

Resistance in the Gaza Strip was markedly different from that on the West Bank. Substantial quantities of weapons were hidden in the Strip after the Egyptian army was defeated in June 1967. Moreover Egypt had allowed the PLO-supported Palestine Liberation Army (PLA) to recruit members in the Gaza Strip, and these soldiers remained at large in refugee camps, poor quarters of Gaza and the dense orange groves. The politicians connected with the Arab National Movement (ANM) encouraged armed resistance and opposed any form of coöperation with the Israeli military authorities. By the end of 1970 the *fida'iyin* controlled the camps and, at night, the towns. Grenades were lobbed into marketplaces to disrupt commerce, and at places where people congregated who worked inside Israel, such as post offices, banks, and buses. The Gaza economy remained paralyzed: pre-war jobs connected with the United Nations Emergency Forces at the Gaza port, the Egyptian government and the PLA had vanished, leaving only seasonal orange picking and offshore fishing. Some 7,000 residents felt compelled to take day-labor jobs inside Israel by March 1968, but others were deterred by the *fida'iyin*.

On January 4, 1971—immediately after a grenade killed two Israeli civilians driving in Gaza—the Israeli military authorities clamped down on the Strip. The mayor, Raghib al-'Alami, was summarily dismissed, followed by the entire Gaza municipality on February 15. Twenty-hour curfews were imposed on refugee camps while Israeli troops made door-to-door searches, and the men from the camps were sometimes forced to stand waist-deep in the Mediterranean Sea while the soldiers pursued their hunt. Three Popular Front (ANM) leaders were killed by Israeli soldiers in early January, and some 12,000 people were deported to detention camps in Sinai, including families of suspects.[24] In July 1971 the army began to "thin out" the refugee camps, demolishing almost forty houses daily in Jabalya camp, which housed 40,000 persons. Many of those who lost their homes were removed to al-Arish in Sinai.[25] The army bulldozed wide streets through the Jabalya and Shati refugee camps in order to seal off and separate each section and to prevent the camps from serving as hiding places for the *fida'iyin*. After UN Secretary General U Thant protested against the demolitions and evacuations, the army temporarily ceased them. By then over 13,000 people had been uprooted.[26]

The guerrilla forces were gradually destroyed through these operations, whose methods further embittered the population against the Israeli forces. When five guerrillas, who had been flushed out of their hideout in Shati Camp, died in a gunbattle in Gaza the night of July 24/25, 1971, several hundred residents assembled at the hospital to recover their bodies and bury them. And a funeral for six *fida'iyin* in Breij Camp erupted into a stone-throwing riot against Israel. But on November 21, 1971, the commanding officer of the Popular Front, Major Ziyad Muhammad al-Husayni, committed suicide while hiding in the house of the newly installed Gaza mayor, Rashad Shawwa.[27] And three weeks later the army killed the deputy commander, 28-year-old Mahmud Bsayli, as he crouched in a concealed bunker in an orange grove.[28] By the end of 1971, the year-long crackdown had caused the death of more than a hundred guerrillas and had broken the backbone of the armed resistance in the Strip.

Municipal Council Elections

The Israeli military authorities reactivated the municipalities on the West Bank and Gaza after June 1967, but supervised them closely and left them with few powers. One Israeli analyst commented that the military government always retained the last word "and when mayors ignore the fact, administrative measures are taken to insure compliance with government policy, such as withholding government financial support (loans, development funds, tax rebates) to the city or withholding various permits and licenses for the city residents."[29] Municipal budgets had to be approved by the military government, as well as lists of permanent municipal staff. The mayors of Jerusalem and Ramallah and the deputy mayor of Jenin were deported to Jordan, and the municipality of Gaza was dismissed—and replaced by Israeli army officers—in early 1971. The residents had to balance their need for indigenous officials against the circumscribed role that these officials could play: there was a fine line between conducting normal business and "collaborating" with the occupier.

Therefore the decision by Rashad Shawwa to accept the mayoralty of Gaza in September 1971 aroused conflicting responses. Although he was appointed by the Israeli military authorities, he stressed that he would not have accepted the post without the endorsement expressed in a petition signed by 6,000 Gaza residents. Moreover, he sought to gain public support by reviving the economy and reducing Gaza's isolation. He opened transportation links across the Jordan bridges to ship Gaza oranges to Iran and the Arab states and to let Gaza students and other residents travel abroad on special *laissez passers*. He attempted to assert his distance from the military authorities by denouncing Israeli statements that the Strip would never be separated from Israel, and by calling on the UN to "rescue and protect" Gaza from Israeli annexation.[30] But he encountered sharp criticism in early 1972 when he supported the plan proposed by King Hussein to federate the East and West Banks, with Gaza serving as Jordan's outlet to the Mediterranean. Pro-Egyptian residents of Gaza opposed Shawwa's attempt to transfer the center of gravity of Gaza politics from Egypt to Jordan, and the influential Shaykh Hashim Khuzundar declaimed: "How can we give ourselves up to a man whose hands are still stained with the blood of our sons?"[31] Moreover, threats were made against Shawwa's life by PFLP militants who remained hidden in the Gaza Strip.

Shawwa's rule was short-lived. After only one year, he was ready to resign, buffeted by denunciations from fellow

Palestinians and pressure from the Israelis. The military government had ordered him to extend the Gaza municipal services to the nearby Shati refugee camp. Shawwa refused to take this step, which might annul the camp dwellers' refugee status, and he thereby gave the Israelis cause to dismiss him on October 22, 1972, and to reinstate direct military rule. Shortly after his dismissal, Shawwa depicted the low morale on the Strip:[32]

The people here are depressed, almost numb from doubts about their future. They want the Israelis to leave. They don't want to become second-class citizens in a foreign land, like the Israeli Arabs. But they're afraid that is what is going to happen to them.

In contrast to Gaza, where the municipal councils had been appointed under Egypt, councils on the West Bank had been elected during the Jordanian period. In December 1971 the Israel government announced that municipal elections would be held in several towns on the West Bank. Elections were long overdue, but the residents feared that participating would seem to legitimize the occupation. Both the Jordan government and the PLO responded to Israel's announcement by calling on residents to boycott the elections.[33] From Beirut, PLO spokesman Kamal Nasir declared that the elections were part of a plot to liquidate the Palestine problem, warning participants that the PLO "will not stand idly by."[34] And the underground Communist newspaper on the West Bank spread the argument that Israel was trying to profit from the residents' hatred of Amman and was posing occupation as the only alternative to Hashimite rule.[35] Another Communist statement distributed in early March 1972 called on the residents "to repudiate the renegades who propose themselves as candidates and to take punitive measures against them."[36]

But was it realistic to boycott the elections? By mid-January 1972, King Hussein withdrew his threat of sanctions against candidates, having decided that a boycott would undermine his supporters on the councils.[37] He still sought to regain control over the West Bank and would have found his position weakened if either supporters of Israeli rule or anti-Jordanian independents won control over the councils. Therefore he urged the notables—with considerable success—to stand for reëlection. Moreover Israel viewed the elections as a test of its credibility and authority. The more the PLO urged the residents to resist, the more the Israelis sought to save face. Many incumbents were compelled to stand for reëlection. Later one resident charged that "the Israelis bribed, threatened and finally forced us to put up candidates."[38]

Elections were held in ten towns in the northern part of the West Bank in late March 1972. Eighty four per cent of the 17,000 eligible voters went to the polls and half of the incumbent mayors were reëlected, notably in Nablus and Tulkarm.[39] Turnout was high because identity cards were stamped: residents feared that they would encounter difficulties in their jobs and in obtaining permits and bridge passes if they failed to vote.

Given the failure of the boycott, the politicians who supported the PLO and the Communist Party reconsidered their position. They decided that instead of adhering to the futile call to boycott, they should urge the voters to "resist" by reëlecting the incumbents in the second round of elections scheduled for April 1972 in thirteen southern towns. Thus, the PLO supporters backed, on the one hand, the conservative mayor Muhammad 'Ali al-Ja'bari in Hebron, and, on the other hand, the radical mayor 'Abd al-Jawad Salih in al-Bireh.[40] This pragmatic shift was supported—after the fact—by the PLO, which never carried out any threats against voters. A memorandum from the West Bank that was publicized favorably at the Palestinian Popular Congress in Cairo argued that the West Bank residents had ensured that pro-Israeli politicians were not elected: "The same municipal councils were elected, purely as municipal councils, and we shall make every effort to ensure that these councils do not acquire any political significance."[41]

Acquiescing to municipal elections on the West Bank was viewed in a different light from accepting Israel's effort to establish new governing bodies in the Gaza Strip. Shortly after dismissing Mayor Shawwa in October 1972, the Israeli military government tried to hold elections for committees in refugee camps and town quarters. These committees were intended to form the basis for a general council that would oversee local affairs in the Strip. Israel called a meeting for February 11, 1973, to elect the chairman of that council. But the meeting was cancelled abruptly when the leading candidate—the chairman of the Shati camp committee— was abducted from his house during the night and killed by the PFLP. The next day, guerrillas shot at Shawwa, who had agreed to chair one of the Gaza neighborhood committees. And six of the eight committees immediately resigned *en masse*.[42] The PFLP distributed leaflets in Gaza denouncing such "collaboration"[43] and no further attempt was made to revive these committees. (The PFLP was estranged from the PLO leadership and sometimes resorted to personal violence eschewed by the PLO itself.)

By the end of 1972, residents defined resistance more in terms of coping with an unpleasant situation than in terms of active, militant operations. Strikes and demonstrations, armed violence and political action had all proved ineffective, since the residents lacked significant external support. Neither the neighboring Arab states nor the PLO had fought or negotiated successfully to release the territories from Israeli control. The only possible tactic appeared to be to maintain the Palestinians' presence in the West Bank and Gaza in the hope of an eventual change in the balance of power. A university student from Nablus urged a foreign correspondent: "Don't be fooled by the surface calm . . . We all believe that what they want ultimately is to throw us out and take our land . . . But we are not going to leave . . . Even if the whole world outside has forgotten us, and all the Arab governments continue to use our cause for their own political ends, if we leave here Palestinians are nowhere and we become non-persons. And this we will not do."[44]

NOTES, CHAPTER 2

1. Kamal Nasir (journalist), Ibrahim Bakr (lawyer) and Faiq Warrad (Communist leader). For a comprehensive list of deportees, see my "Israeli Deportation of Palestinians from the West Bank and the Gaza Strip, 1967–1978," *Journal of Palestine Studies*, number 30, winter 1979, pp. 101–31, and number 31, spring 1979, pp. 81–112.
2. For descriptions of the West Bank between 1948 and 1967, see Aqil Abidi, *Jordan: A Political Study, 1948–1957* (New York: Asia Publishing House, 1965); Amnon Cohen, "The Jordanian Communist Party in the West Bank, 1950–1960," in *The USSR and the Middle East*, ed. Michael Confino and Shimon Shamir (New York: John Wiley and Sons, 1973); Amnon Cohen, "Political Parties in the West Bank under the Hashemite Regime," in *Palestinian Arab Politics*, ed. Moshe Ma'oz (Jerusalem: Jerusalem Academic Press, 1975); Naseer H. Aruri, *Jordan: A Study in Political Development, 1921–1965* (The Hague: Martinus Nijhoff, 1972); and Shaul Mishal, *West Bank/East Bank: The Palestinians in Jordan, 1949–1967* (New Haven: Yale University Press, 1978).
3. *Al-Dustur* (Amman), August 16, 1967; *The New York Times*, July 26, 1967. For an extended analysis of the initial period of occupation, see my monograph, *Israel's Occupation of the West Bank: The First Two Years* (Santa Monica, Calif.: RAND Research Monograph, 1970).
4. Reproduced in *International Documents on Palestine, 1967*, ed. Fuad A. Jabber (Beirut: Institute for Palestine Studies, 1970), pp. 682–86.
5. The idea was proposed, separately, by Shaykh Muhammad 'Ali al-Ja'bari, mayor of Hebron; Aziz Shehadeh, a lawyer in Ramallah; and Dr. Hamdi Taji al-Faruqi of Ramallah.
6. For details on the lawyers' and teachers' strikes, see my *Israel's Occupation*, pp. 17–19 and 47–57.
7. The teachers' statement issued on August 15, 1967. Quoted in *al-Dustur* (Amman), September 2, 1967.

8. *The New York Times*, June 6, 1968.
9. *Jerusalem Post*, October 25, 1968, and Israel radio broadcast (Arabic), November 1, 1968. *The New York Times*, October 24, 1968, described the atmosphere in Ramallah: "A week of rising tension stimulated by student demonstrations culminated today in violence, arrests and a curfew in Ramallah . . . The move came after 400 girls . . . had marched into the center of Ramallah carrying pictures of Nasser. . . . Shouting anti-Israel slogans and chanting 'We are all fedayeen,' . . . the girls carried what had been daily schoolyard protests into the downtown area. Israeli officials said that when the girls began throwing stones and spitting at Israeli soldiers, the occupying forces turned the high-pressure hoses on them and ordered the curfew."
10. *Jerusalem Post*, April 16, 1968, and my *Israel's Occupation*, pp. 66–8.
11. Contained in a letter submitted by the Jordan government to the United Nations, June 3, 1968, UN Document S/8609.
12. Hamdi Kan'an, quoted in *The New York Times*, February 7, 1969.
13. *Jerusalem Post*, September 20, 1967, and Israel radio broadcast October 20, 1967.
14. David Caute in the *Manchester Guardian Weekly*, July 18, 1970.
15. During September 1970, Israel rounded up 450 residents of the West Bank and Gaza, including eighty women, as apparent counter-hostages, and sent six prominent residents to Lebanon to warn the Popular Front of the consequences if it harmed the hostages on the planes. See my "Israeli Deportations," part I, pp. 110 and 130.
16. *The New York Times*, September 28, 1970.
17. Quoted in *The New York Times*, September 19, 1970.
18. *Le Monde*, November 18, 1970.
19. *Al-Quds*, December 7, 1970; also his statement in *al-Quds*, October 22, 1970.
20. *Le Monde*, November 18, 1970.
21. *Al Quds*, October 16, 1970.
22. See also the statement by Dr. Hamdi Taji al-Faruqi to *The New York Times*, September 19, 1970; Abu Shilayah in *al-Quds*, December 29, 1970 and January 6, 1971; and a report in *The New Middle East* (London), June 1971. These intellectuals (who included the teacher Ibrahim Duaybis, the poet Samira Khatib, and the journalists Yusif Nasr and Jamil Hamad) were sharply critical of the traditional leadership as well as the Israeli authorities: *The New York Times*, December 6, 1970, quoted from a manifesto that was circulating privately on the West Bank— "The regional tribal regime in Amman . . . which prepared the defeat in June [1967], has learned nothing and, indeed, confirms every day its insistence on fighting the national wishes, defeating and humiliating our nation. . . . The traditional leadership in the occupied territories has proved in its attitudes that the money they receive as salaries from Amman, their personal and private interests, are more important to them than their allegiance to the cause and benefit of their people."

23. This perspective gained support in private. One professional from Ramallah commented to the *Washington Post*, July 19, 1971: "If I want to be an extremist, I will say that the whole of Palestine is my land. Maybe this is the feeling of most Palestinians. But as a practical matter, the partition of 1947 or a modification of the partition plan whereby every Palestinian would have the right of return and those who choose not to return would be compensated—I think that would be acceptable."
24. *The Christian Science Monitor*, February 3, 1971.
25. *The New York Times*, August 20, 1971.
26. *The New York Times*, August 31, 1971.
27. The suicide of Husayni remains problematic. Shawwa was apparently negotiating with the Israelis for the amnesty and deportation of Husayni and some other *fida'iyin*, and had allowed him to hide in his basement. The suicide may have been prompted by a deadlock in the negotiations, or it may not have been a suicide at all.
28. *The New York Times*, December 18, 1971; see also the *Washington Post*, December 16, 1971.
29. Nimrod Raphaeli, "Military Government in the Occupied Territories: The Israeli View," *The Middle East Journal*, Spring 1969, p. 190.
30. *Washington Post*, April 28, 1972.
31. *Davar*, August 14, 1971; also see Khuzundar's comments quoted in *Davar*, August 21, 1972.
32. *The New York Times*, October 24, 1972.
33. *The New York Times*, December 12, 1971.
34. *Al-Anwar* (Beirut), February 11, 1972.
35. *Al-Watan* newspaper, quoted in *al-Ittihad*, December 7, 1971.
36. Issued in the name of the "Popular Resistance Front in the West Bank" and quoted in *al-Dustur* (Amman), March 12, 1972; see also an article in *al-Watan*, reprinted in *al-Muharrir* (Beirut), March 29, 1972.
37. *The New York Times*, January 12, 1972.
38. *The Christian Science Monitor*, December 11, 1972.
39. Statistics in the *Jerusalem Post*, April 4, 1972.
40. Statistics in the *Jerusalem Post*, May 9, 1972. A significant change did occur in Ramallah, where the former Ba'thi lawyer Karim Khalaf defeated the incumbent mayor.
41. *Fateh* (Beirut), April 12, 1972, quoted in *Journal of Palestine Studies*, number 4, summer 1972, p. 160.
42. *Times* (London), February 13, 1973; *Yediot Ahronot*, February 18 and 19, 1973.
43. Three armed guerrillas were killed on March 9, 1973, in a bunker under the floor of Dr. Rashad Musmar's home in Gaza. They had Popular Front leaflets, including some that threatened collaborators. The guerrillas included Muhammad al-Aswad (known as Ché Guevara), who had been sought for three years. The doctor was arrested and his house was demolished.
44. Quoted in *The Christian Science Monitor*, December 11, 1972.

Chapter 3

THE REVIVAL OF THE
NATIONAL MOVEMENT

After the rupture of Palestinian-Jordanian relations in 1970, some individuals on the West Bank began to articulate the concept of establishing an independent state in the territories occupied by Israel in 1967. Both Jordan and the PLO denounced that idea, and its proponents were accused of betraying the Palestinians' land and heritage. However, the PLO itself began to revise its political strategy in the early 1970s. In January 1973, the Palestine National Council decided in secret to establish a National Front on the West Bank and Gaza in order to help the residents overcome their demoralization, to demonstrate that the territories were not a political vacuum that could be filled by either Jordan or Israel, and to provide a political base for a future independent régime.

During the early 1970s, Yasir Arafat did not expect the residents of the territories to assume an active military role in the struggle for liberation. Rather, he felt it was important for the Palestinians to remain on the land, awaiting their release from occupation: "merely holding out for a day is a small victory," he stated.[1] Nayef Hawatmeh, head of the Democratic Front for the Liberation of Palestine, urged the Palestinians to intensify their struggle inside the occupied territories, but he criticized those who voiced slogans and "revolutionary phrases like 'Haifa before Hebron' or 'Jaffa before Jerusalem' "[2] without developing a coherent strategy to achieve their aims. Nevertheless, Hawatmeh felt that liberation would only be achieved by overthrowing the pro-Jordanians in the territories and inflicting a military defeat on

Israel, not by negotiations.

The Popular Front leader, George Habash, went a step further by rejecting any consideration of accepting a state in part of Palestine. Habash termed such ideas imperialist conspiracies to "liquidate the Palestine cause," and argued that the national front in "occupied Palestine" should struggle against Israel itself, not only the occupation.[3] In contrast, the Jordanian Communist Party formulated a proposal for a national front in the occupied territories that would seek the liberation specifically of the lands taken in June 1967 and the evacuation of Israeli forces on the basis of the UN Security Council resolutions.[4] The Communist formulation was more limited in scope and explicit in its negotiating strategy than the other groups within the PLO were willing to be at that time.

The residents of the West Bank were beginning to be receptive to the idea of renewing their nationalist activities, despite Israeli military pressure on them to remain silent and their perception of the Arab states' weakness relative to Israel. The political debate in Beirut affected the politicians and intellectuals on the West Bank and Gaza. And powerful emotions were aroused when Israeli commandos assassinated three PLO leaders in Beirut on April 10, 1973.[5] Those killed included Kamal Nasir, a well known journalist and activist, who was one of the first persons deported from the West Bank. Leading citizens attended the memorial service for him at Bir Zeit, and the Arabic newspapers in Jerusalem were filled with bereavement notices and militant editorials. The independent, nationalist paper *al-Fajr* editorialized:[6]

They died because they loved their homeland and were willing to die for it ... Mothers of Palestine, do not weep over the deaths of heroes, for their deaths will bring about the growth of other men who will follow these heroes ... The anguish accompanying their deaths roused the Palestinians to hope and cries of battle.

The Israeli authorities briefly arrested the editor of *al-Fajr* and the assistant editor, on charges of evading censorship and inciting revolution.[7] The two other Arabic newspapers, *al-Quds* and *al-Sha'b*, then defied censorship to run editorials calling their arrests a blow to the freedom of the press.[8]

Tension increased when about 200 West Bankers were arrested just prior to Israel's twenty-fifth anniversary, May 7, 1973. Despite the arrests, some of the Arabs marked the anniversary by distributing pamphlets and writing slogans on walls that denounced occupation and asserted Palestinian national rights. Moreover, leading residents began to speak out publicly on political issues, despite the total ban on political activity and the military governor's frequent warnings to the mayors that they must restrict themselves to municipal affairs.[9] In July 1973, 107 prominent citizens of the West Bank and Gaza signed an appeal to the UN Secretary General that demanded an end to the occupation and reaffirmed "their right to self-determination and to sovereignty."[10] But the politicians remained divided as to the proper definition of "self-determination", as did the PLO activists outside. Did it refer to the 1947 partition plan, to the 1948–67 cease fire line, or to all of Palestine? Did it involve accepting the existence of Israel alongside a Palestinian state, or did it mean accepting a separate state only as a stage toward the liberation of all of Palestine?

These issues were not fully resolved by the time the Palestine National Front was established in August 1973.[11] The PNF was a coalition of political groups and independent politicians, including supporters of Fatah, the Democratic Front, the Communist Party, the Ba'th Party and, for a short period, the Popular Front. Proclaiming the National Front "an inseparable part of the Palestinian national movement represented in the Palestine Liberation Organization," its thirteen point manifesto issued on August 15 called for the safeguarding of the legitimate rights of the

Palestinian people, and stressed their rights to self-determination on their land and to the return to their homes. It rejected plans to establish a separate entity in the territories under Israeli control, as well as rejecting the Allon Plan and King Hussein's federation proposal. The manifesto called for the defense of the land, economy, culture, and holy places against the occupier and concluded that the National Front must increase the self-confidence of the people, raise the level of their struggle against the occupation, eliminate the claim that there is a vacuum in the occupied territories, and assert the unity of the struggle of the Palestinian people everywhere. At the insistence of the Communists, reference to the goal of a democratic secular state was deleted from the final draft of the manifesto. Even though the Communist Party did not persuade the other groups to mention the 1967 borders explicitly, the Popular Front activists feared "liquidationist" tendencies within the PNF and tended to withhold their support from it.

The first test of the PNF's strength came with the elections in Jerusalem for the Israeli Federation of Labor (Histadrut), held in September 1973. The Front called on workers to boycott the elections, because they would consolidate the occupation.[12] The PNF activists were supported in this position by the pro-Jordanian politicians, who also opposed Israel's annexation of Jerusalem, and the boycott was markedly successful. The real measure of the PNF's strength came after the October War.

The October War

The October War of 1973 broke out just as the Palestinian activists were trying to regroup themselves and build a solid political framework in the occupied territories. Two organizers later commented: "The activity of the Palestine National Front really got underway and its influence became

significant after the October War, as a result of the nationalist resurgence initiated by the war" and even though political organizing was "no simple task" in the occupied territories.[13]

The ability of the Egyptian and Syrian military to coördi-
nate, launch and sustain a lengthy battle against the seem-
ingly invincible Israeli forces raised morale throughout the
Arab world, even though the war ended with Israeli troops
astride the Suez Canal and controlling additional territory
on the Golan Heights. The war had an extraordinary psy-
chological impact in the occupied territories.[14] The mayor of
al-Bireh exulted: "For the first time we feel ecstacy, we
sense victory. We have achieved a major step towards liberation." And a Nablus dignitary affirmed, more cautiously:[15]

> To conquer Israel is impossible, but the myth of Israeli
> might has been broken. The impression that Arabs cannot
> fight has been terminated. If we lose this time, we will lose
> with honor. And we will be back again and again.

The heightened nationalism and renewed optimism did
not cause the Palestinians to escalate their political demands. The feeling of self-confidence and restored pride
seemed to enable people to adopt an increasingly realistic
approach. The politicians on the West Bank and Gaza
coupled their demand for international recognition of the
PLO as the sole representative of the Palestinian people
with an increasingly explicit demand for an independent
state on the West Bank and Gaza.[16] They also urged the
PLO to attend the Peace Conference in Geneva if invited,
and counseled the Palestinian leadership to beware of "sen-
timental" or "adventurist" approaches since the current international context meant that not all of the Palestinians'
strategic aims could be realized.[17]

The PNF's growing influence was demonstrated by its

ability to persuade the conservative Supreme Muslim Council in Jerusalem to issue a statement on December 3, 1973, backing the Algiers summit conference's recognition of the PLO. This was a sharp blow to King Hussein's supporters, and angered the Israeli government.

Israel's first effort to stem the nationalist protests came on December 10, 1973, when the government deported eight leaders of the PNF to Jordan. They included the mayor of al-Bireh, three Communists, three professionals from Nablus, and the member of the Muslim Council who had engineered its pro-PLO statement the previous week. The deportations triggered widespread protests on the West Bank. The military governor closed down Bir Zeit College for two weeks, and arrested eleven women during a vigil in Jerusalem.[18] *Al-Quds* commented that Israel had returned to the policy of "the big stick, fright and insecurity."[19]

As a reflection of the strengthened criticism of Israeli rule, Arab participation was minimal in the Israeli municipal council elections in Jerusalem on December 31, 1973: 18 per cent of the eligible Arab voters had participated in 1969, but only 10 per cent voted in 1973. An East Jerusalem leader underlined the reasons for the boycott:[20]

> If you have not understood yet, you had better understand now: When the whole Arab world is demanding that Jerusalem be returned to the Arabs, we here cannot take part in the elections and vote for parties which call for a unified Jerusalem under Israeli rule.

Meanwhile, the Jordan government mounted a vigorous campaign to regain influence on the West Bank. Already, on the eve of the October War, the King had released 750 political prisoners and amnestied 2,500 others who had been blacklisted since 1970–71. The editor of *al-Quds* praised Hussein for this gesture, which would help to bind the wounds of Black September.[21] After the October War, Jordan entered into discussions with US Secretary of State Henry Kissinger, who was negotiating disengagements on the Egypt-Israel and Syria-Israel fronts. King Hussein hoped to join the negotiations and to prove to the West Bank residents that Jordan, rather than the PLO, could release them from the Israeli occupation. He felt that he could rely for support on the Muslim leadership in Jerusalem and most of the chambers of commerce and municipalities. Therefore, the dissent expressed by the Muslim Council in December 1973 appeared particularly dangerous. *Al-Quds* newspaper and Shaykh Ja'bari of Hebron remained the staunchest supporters of the King.[22] Ja'bari was repeatedly attacked by pro-PLO editor Yusif Nasr in *al-Fajr*, and the pro-Hashimites were increasingly on the defensive. Tension between the two camps peaked in February 1974 when Nasr vanished and Ja'bari's chauffeur was indicated for kidnapping him.[23] By this turn to violence the King's supporters risked weakening the Arab position and helping Israel divide and rule. But the kidnapping remained an isolated occurrence.

During the spring of 1974 the PNF became increasingly active as it rode the crest of the nationalist wave. Some 500 public figures gathered at the East Jerusalem YMCA in early March to call for Palestinian self-determination, protests were voiced against the demolition of houses, and prisoners held a strike in Nablus in February and March that was supported by Arab delegations to the Red Cross offices.[24] Acts of sabotage also escalated, climaxing with the murder of an Israeli taxi driver in Jerusalem in mid-April.[25] The PNF itself remained a tactical alliance, encompassing diverse groups and interests. Supporters of the Popular Front had withdrawn from the PNF when the PNF began to support the ideas of a limited territorial settlement and participation in the Geneva negotiations, since the Popular Front still insisted on a long term guerrilla struggle aimed at eliminating Israel. But the Popular Front's defection did not materially weaken the PNF and, in fact, the PNF gained broad popular support.

In an attempt to crush the PNF, the Israeli military authorities arrested over 150 political activists in May 1974 and detained more than 300 people by July. This large scale round-up affected particularly the Communist leaders and activists. The party head, Suleiman Najjab (who was also number two in the PNF and had been underground since 1967) was arrested, along with local organizers from Bethlehem, Ramallah and Nablus.[26]

An Israeli journalist reported that the detentions had been designed to instill fear, obtain information and discourage others from protesting, but that the arrests themselves had exacerbated tension and fueled protest.[27] Palestinian women held hunger strikes at the Red Cross offices and municipalities. The Arabic press expressed strong support for the June 1974 program outlined by the PLO's Palestine National Council, which endorsed the establishment of a "national authority" on "every part of the Palestine territory that is liberated." And al-Fajr did not hesitate to address an editorial to US President Richard Nixon, during his tour of the Middle East, in which it reasserted the Palestinians' right to self-determination, the representativeness of the PLO, and the need for "complete Israeli withdrawal from the territories occupied in 1967."[28] Moreover, the Communist underground newspaper, al-Watan, managed to reappear in September after a hiatus of several months.[29] The trials of the Catholic Archbishop Hilarion Capucci, who was accused of smuggling arms, and of Bashir Barghuthi, a Communist activist who was the first important detainee to be tried, attracted considerable attention on the West Bank and abroad, and were written up in detail in the Arabic newspapers. The first anniversary of the October War was "celebrated" with Palestinian flags and anti-Israel slogans.[30] The crackdown on the PNF had apparently served to widen its appeal, as nationalist fervor spread in the occupied territories.

The Rabat Summit

The contest between the pro-Hashimite and pro-PLO politicians for the allegiance of the people on the West Bank had been muted since February 1974. But it resumed in the weeks before the Arab League summit conference in Rabat (October 26–29, 1974). Jordan's adherents wanted the summit to name King Hussein as the negotiator on behalf of the West Bank, and the PNF activists sought endorsement of the PLO at Rabat. The decision was critically important, since it could determine whether the West Bank would be reabsorbed into Jordan or would serve as the base for an independent Palestinian state.

Seven West Bank residents who had served in the Jordanian parliament met in Amman on October 21 and signed a petition that asserted Jordan's "legitimate constitutional right" to the West Bank and Jerusalem. The petition also noted that more than half of the Palestinians lived on the two banks of the Jordan, thereby reinforcing the Jordanian claim to represent them both, but suggested that a plebiscite be held so that the Palestinians could choose the form of rule they preferred.[31] Soon afterwards, the cars of two leading supporters of Hussein—Anwar Khatib and Anwar Nusseibeh—were firebombed in Jerusalem, a clear threat against the King's men by Palestinian militants.[32]

In early October PNF activists began to collect signatures on a petition to endorse the PLO as the sole representative of the Palestinian people and to support the concept of a Palestinian "national authority" on the West Bank and Gaza.[33] The document contained the signatures of nearly 180 residents of the occupied territories, including mayors, Muslim and Christian leaders, and prominent individuals in professional, women's and labor organizations.[34] The petition had a major impact on the Rabat summit conference, because Arafat used it as proof of the widespread support for the

PLO on the West Bank and Gaza. The summit set aside Jordan's claims and conferred the exclusive representational role on the PLO. For the first time the PLO could aspire to international diplomatic status and begin to devise a serious negotiating strategy.

The public on the West Bank praised the Rabat decision. "Revolution until victory" was inscribed by youths on the walls of Jerusalem. And the Israeli cabinet resolved to crack down again on PNF activists.[35] The editor of *al-Sha'b* was deported to Lebanon on November 4, 1974, for helping to organize the petition as well as for writing militant editorials. Three other activists, including the deputy mayor of Halhul, were also banished to Lebanon that night.

A week later, Arafat's speech at the UN General Assembly sparked an outpouring of demonstrations and strikes on the West Bank. Students took to the streets in the main towns on November 16: 2,000 pupils demonstrated in Jenin and, when Israeli soldiers killed a teenage girl, thousands of residents of Jenin attended her funeral. The sit-ins and demonstrations continued to spread, even affecting small villages. On November 19, 1974, a new stage of civil disobedience was reached when a business strike crippled the Old City of Jerusalem and, the following day, shuttered the shops in Ramallah and al-Bireh.[36] That night, five men were deported to Lebanon, including a member of the Ramallah municipality, a leader of its Chamber of Commerce and the president of Bir Zeit College, Dr. Hanna Nasir. Nasir's deportation led to further demonstrations at Bir Zeit, and youths clashed with the police in Jerusalem after Friday prayers at al-Aqsa mosque.[37] Thus, demonstrations that were originally triggered by Arafat's speech took on their own momentum during the following weeks.

The rest of the winter the West Bank remained tense but relatively quiet. The twelve year sentence meted out to Archbishop Capucci aroused anger, but there was relief at the acquittal of Barghuthi in February 1975. In fact, that acquittal had an ironic result: given the difficulty in gaining evidence against the Communist detainees, the military authorities swiftly deported the Communist leaders who had been held since 1974, including Suleiman Najjab. Barghuthi then became the effective head of the party on the West Bank[38] and subsequently assumed the editorship of *al-Fajr*.

The initial optimism on the West Bank and Gaza after the October War, buoyed by the PLO's successes at Rabat and the UN, wore off as time passed and the fundamental situation did not improve. The deteriorating conditions in Lebanon in the spring and summer of 1975 and the second disengagement agreement concluded between Egypt and Israel in September 1975 caused further strains. The PLO was still unable to lever its new diplomatic status into a dialogue with the US government or an invitation to Geneva. In fact, a secret American-Israeli annex to the Sinai accord committed the US government to open such negotiations only if the PLO accepted UN Security Council Resolution 242. Some Palestinians feared that the Popular Front had been correct in asserting that moderating their position would only cause pressure for further concessions. Others were anxious that negotiations would take so long that the territories would be strangled by settlements and absorbed into the Israeli economy by the time talks would be concluded. Nevertheless, residents expressed pride in their renewed expression of nationalism and hoped that it would be translated soon into political deeds.

NOTES, CHAPTER 3

1. Interview in *Filastin al-Thawra*, August 1, 1973, translated in the *Journal of Palestine Studies*, number 9, autumn 1973, p. 192.
2. Interview in *al-Nahar* (Beirut), August 17, 1973, *ibid.*, p. 201.
3. Interview in *al-Akhbar* (Beirut), August 4, 1973, *ibid.*, pp. 196–7.
4. *Al-Watan*, February 1973, quoted in *al-Ittihad*, March 2, 1973; see also

Yediot Ahronot, February 20, 1973, and *al-Ittihad*, March 9, 1973.

5. The two others were Kamal Adwan of the Fatah executive committee, in charge of guerrilla activity in the occupied territories, and Muhammad Yusif Najjar, chairman of the PLO's political department. Documents seized in Adwan's apartment apparently led to the arrest of numerous suspected guerrillas in the occupied territories the night of April 11/12 and uncovered plans for actions on Israeli independence day, May 7; *The New York Times*, April 13, 1973, and *The Christian Science Monitor*, April 24, 1973.

6. April 14, 1973. See also the editorials in *al-Quds* and *al-Sha'b* on April 11, 1973; *The New York Times*, April 17, 1973; and the poem written by Kamal Nasir's mother and printed (without being submitted to the Israeli censor) in *al-Fajr* on April 14, 1973:

   My son, Kamal . . .
   We see you in every youth. . . .
   'I will not die today'
   I am a revolutionary . . .
   My death fans flames . . .
   Your fate is between the spears
   Your death is a symbol to all youth . . .
   And I will hear your voice in all the cities
   Cry
   'We will remain despite our non-existence'
   We will raise our dead
   And we will raise our flag with pride.

7. *The New York Times*, April 17, 1973; *Yediot Ahronot*, April 25, 1973.

8. *Ha'Aretz*, April 20, 1973.

9. *Yediot Ahronot*, May 9, 1973; *Ha'Aretz*, June 27, 1973.

10. The mayors of Nablus, Tulkarm, al-Bireh, Ramallah, Khan Yunis and Rafah signed the statement as well as representatives of religious bodies and labor and professional societies. *Journal of Palestine Studies*, number 9, autumn 1973, pp. 187–9 gives the complete text and list of names. Another appeal was submitted to UN Secretary General Kurt Waldheim in August 1973 during his visit to Israel, and a hunger strike was held during that visit, which was supported by the women's societies and Red Crescent societies; *al-Ittihad*, August 31, 1973, and *Israleft*, number 24, September 17, 1973.

11. Quoted in full in *al-Ittihad*, September 7, 1973. Commentaries on the formation of the PNF were provided by deported activists Arabi Awwad and Jirius Qawwas (Wafa news agency interview, May 29, 1974, translated in *Journal of Palestine Studies*, number 12, summer 1974, pp. 164–5) and Dr. Abd al-Aziz (*MERIP Reports*, number 50).

12. Pamphlets attacking Muhammad Abu Shilbaya, quoted in *al-Ittihad*, September 10, 1973; *Ha'Aretz*, September 11, 1973; *al-Watan* editorial denouncing Shaykh Ja'bari and Abu Shilbaya, quoted in *al-Ittihad*, September 21, 1973. Abu Shilbaya published a weekly newspaper, *Sawt*

al-Jamahir, from September to November 1973 that supported Arab participation in the Histadrut and Israeli municipal council elections in Jerusalem and called for peaceful coexistence, full mutual recognition between Israel and Palestine, and open borders. By then he had parted company with both Yusif Nasr, whose al-Fajr newspaper backed the National Front, and Mahmud Abu Zuluf of al-Quds, who had returned to a pro-Jordanian posture.

13. Awwad and Qawwas, Wafa interview, May 29, 1974, translated in *Journal of Palestine Studies*, number 12, summer 1974, pp. 164–5.
14. During the war itself people kept a low profile, refraining from working in Israel and, as Rashad Shawwa commented, anxious because they "have experienced very drastic measures during the last six years." But they clung to every word of the radio news bulletins. *Times* (London), October 15, 1973; *The New York Times*, October 9, 1973.
15. Both quotations from the *Times* (London), October 15, 1973.
16. See the early November 1973 proclamations by the PNF and the Jordan Communist Party, reprinted in *al-Ittihad*, November 20, 1973.
17. Message sent to the PLO on December 1, 1973, as reported in *Ha'Aretz*, December 4, 1973; *al-Nahar* (Beirut), December 17, 1973 as translated in *Journal of Palestine Studies*, number 11, spring 1974, pp. 187–91; *al-Ittihad*, February 19, 1974.
18. *Ha'Aretz*, December 16, 1973.
19. Editorial quoted in *Ha'Aretz*, December 14, 1973.
20. *Ha'Aretz*, January 8, 1974.
21. *Al-Quds* editorial of September 20, 1973, quoted in the *Times* (London), September 21, 1973.
22. *Ha'Aretz*, January 22, 1974.
23. *Jerusalem Post*, February 10, 1974; *Ma'ariv*, February 13, 1974; *al-Hamishmar*, February 14, 1974; *Davar*, May 20, 1974.
24. *Ma'ariv*, March 10, 1974.
25. *Davar*, April 18, 1974.
26. *Davar*, May 14, 1974; *Ha'Aretz*, May 15, 1974; *Zu Haderech*, May 15, 1974.
27. *Davar*, July 14, 1974.
28. Reported by Wafa press agency, June 19, 1974, translated in *Journal of Palestine Studies*, number 13, autumn 1974, pp. 171–2.
29. *Davar*, September 23, 1974.
30. Israel radio broadcast, October 6, 1974.
31. *Al-Dustur* (Amman), October 22, 1974; *al-Nahar* (Beirut), October 23, 1974.
32. Voice of Palestine broadcast (Beirut), October 26, 1974.
33. *Jerusalem Post*, October 2, 1974. The petition may have actually been drafted outside the occupied territories, with the names appended to it.
34. In an interview in *al-Ahram* (Cairo), published November 8, 1974, Arafat said there were 168 signatures, but *al-Nahar* (Beirut), October 23, 1974, reported 180 signatures and listed the main points in the petition.

35. *Davar*, October 31, 1974; *Ha'Aretz*, October 29, 1974, reported several "inflammatory" editorials; and *Yediot Ahronot*, November 4, 1974, noted the graffiti.
36. *Ha'Aretz*, November 21, 1974.
37. *The New York Times*, November 22, 1974; Israel radio broadcast, November 22, 1974. *Ha'aretz*, November 21, 1974, and *Davar*, November 22, 1974, reported that the military government had banned residents and merchandise from Ramallah and al-Bireh from crossing the Allenby Bridge to the East Bank and had sealed shut four shops in those towns. *Davar*, November 28, 1974, added that the authorities were considering closing *al-Fajr*.
38. The majority of the members of the Communist Party from the West Bank voted to separate their branch (renamed the Palestine Communist Party) from the Jordan CP, at a meeting in Amman in March 1975. Barghuthi opposed that severance but the *de facto* separation of the two sections continued.

Chapter 4

CONSOLIDATING THE
NATIONAL MOVEMENT

Following the establishment of the Palestine National Front in 1973 and the upsurge in nationalist activities in 1974, the national movement surmounted major challenges during 1975 and 1976. In the autumn of 1975 Israeli Defense Minister Shimon Peres proposed a limited autonomy plan for the West Bank and Gaza that was sharply criticized by the nationalist leaders. The public expressed its rejection of Israeli policies by waves of strikes and acts of civil disobedience throughout the West Bank. Then the Israeli government announced that new municipal council elections would be held in April 1976. The PNF responded by organizing a political drive that swept its activists into office. That campaign's success marked a high point in Palestinian politics on the West Bank.

Peres unveiled his "civil administration" plan at a meeting with the municipality of Beit Jala on October 20, 1975. Peres was known to seek a federation between Israel and the territories that would leave Israel in control of defense, foreign affairs and finance. His self-rule plan was never clearly articulated, but it included enhancing the powers of the municipalities and placing Arab officials in charge of administrative offices in the territories. It would eventually accord the municipalities and departments authority over civil matters throughout the West Bank and Gaza. When Israel reinstated an Arab municipal council in Gaza three days later, once again under Rashad Shawwa, and held village council elections on the West Bank that fall, these steps seemed to mesh with Peres' plan and to attempt to implant a pliable indigenous leadership.

Peres may have thought that the Palestinians' demoralization after the Sinai accord and their concern about the strife in Lebanon would make them accept any alternative to the *status quo*. But an Israeli journalist stated bluntly: "The Arab public regard this plan as eyewash, since the Israeli government will maintain its control and the autonomy will be false."[1] He also raised pointed questions about its substance:[2]

> When we talk about expanding the powers of the municipalities we must ask ourselves if the municipality of Hebron is to be able to take and implement decisions affecting the mosque of Ibrahim? Will the municipality of Tulkarm be free to take a decision on whether the electricity company is to be attached to Israel or detached from it? When a senior Arab official is appointed Director-General of the Ministry of Labor in the occupied area, will he be responsible for the movement of workers from the areas to Israel? And in whose interest? Will the Arab Director-General of Communications be able to decide how many lines will be given to the Egged [bus] Company in the occupied areas? ...
> [Arabs] believe it is not possible to make any compromise settlements with the occupation and that there are only two possibilities—either it continues or it does not—and everything else is merely a meaningless playing with words.

To these queries, one Palestinian added a vital question about control over land:[3]

> What say would an Arab administration have ... over the question of Jewish settlements on its territory? What powers would it have in relation to abandoned Arab property and the repatriation of its owners?

But few Palestinians deigned to raise such questions: most dismissed the proposal out of hand. Hilmi Hanun, the long time mayor of Tulkarm, stated flatly that "civil administration in the shadow of occupation is against our interest ... We do not think about civil administration but about complete [Israeli] thdrawal from the occupied lands."[4] *Al-Fajr* polled 500 residents and published the statements of 70 people, ranging from the president of the Supreme Muslim Council to the mayors of Nablus and Ramallah, and leading elder statesmen, merchants and professionals. The Nablus dignitary Hikmat al-Masri argued: "The very idea of 'autonomy' in the occupied territories is an insult to the dignity of the Palestinian people ... and we refuse it with all our strength."[5] When leading residents of Gaza linked their criticism of Peres' plan to their opposition to Shawwa for agreeing to serve as mayor, Shawwa was compelled to respond that his reappointment was not linked in any way to the Israeli proposal.[6]

The solid wall of opposition to the Peres plan effectively spelled its demise. By mid-November 1975 one Palestinian editor wondered why Peres even continued to discuss the plan and noted wryly that Peres had little choice, since he could never accept the only clear alternative: "recognition of the right of the Palestinian people to self-determination."[7]

Even as they denounced the "self-rule" plan, many political leaders called on the PLO to accept explicitly the goal of an independent state on the West Bank and the Gaza Strip. Their statements reflected frustration with the vagueness of PLO political formulae and fear that the PLO leaders would not grasp the diplomatic opportunities that had opened up following the October War. The West Bank politicians' views were reflected in editorials in *al-Fajr* and *al-Quds* that urged the Palestinian leadership to capitalize on the gains that it had already won, support the UN resolutions, and join multilateral negotiations in Geneva, chaired by the US and Soviet governments.[8] One such editorial welcomed the invitation by the UN Security Council to the PLO to participate in its January 1976 debate on Palestine and urged the PLO to give specific answers to the diplomats' questions about the "practical application of the right of self-determination" and the territorial limits of a future Palestine state. The editorial argued that a favorable UN Security Council resolution would provide critical support for PLO participation in Geneva, despite American and Israeli opposition.[9]

More pointedly, the underground Communist newspaper requested the PLO to "abandon the slogan of a democratic secular state" and adopt a "realistic program for a just settlement" that would take into account "the real givens of the current Palestinian and Arab situation and the regional and world balance of forces." It concluded:[10]

[The PLO must work] for the reconvening of the Geneva Conference and its participation as a party in it within the scope of the UN resolutions and on the basis of the political need to reclaim the Arab lands occupied since 1967, to stop the tragedy of the Palestinian refugee people, and to start to build a Palestinian national structure which safeguards for our people their special national identity.

But the PLO did not adopt such specific policies in its public statements. At the United Nations, its spokesmen held to general principles, such as the right to self-determination, and did not specify the territorial limits of a Palestinian state. The PLO's grassroots supporters in Lebanon were still too militant to accept the idea of a state confined to the West Bank and Gaza. And Palestinian leaders apparently feared that making such a statement would alienate their mass base while still not gaining them a seat at the Geneva negotiating table. In any event, the United States vetoed the Security Council resolution on Palestinian rights and the real negotiations continued to bypass the Geneva forum.

Civil Disobedience

During the fall of 1975, demonstrations and assemblies on the West Bank marked special anniversaries, starting with Balfour Declaration Day on November 2. A student strike began at Bir Zeit and Bethlehem Universities the next day that lasted for ten days and spread to almost all the secondary schools on the West Bank. Most of the students remained on the school grounds, where they drew up petitions at assemblies and chanted such slogans as "Palestine is Arab" and "Freedom for Palestine." Some students spilled into the streets of Ramallah, Jenin, Jericho and Nablus, where they erected barriers of stones and burned tires. The Israeli military authorities closed down several schools, levied I£4000–5000 ($550–700) fines on many students, and warned school principals and town mayors that they would be held responsible for maintaining order. The military imposed a curfew briefly on Ramallah and al-Bireh on November 15, but demonstrations broke out in the southern towns of Hebron and Halhul on November 16. The rallies subsided by the end of the month, after the UN debates on Palestine were completed. The students felt that they had made their point about Palestinian representation in negotiations and had expressed clearly their opposition to the Peres plan. The heavy fines and pervasive military presence also discouraged further demonstrations.

But another upsurge in civil disobedience began in the Nablus district in December 1975 and spread throughout the West Bank in early 1976. The uprising had multiple causes, both local and international: the establishment of a settlement by the Gush Emunim movement near Nablus in early December 1975 (initially at Sebastia but later moved to Kaddum);[11] the American veto of the UN Security Council resolution on Palestine in January 1976;[12] further land expropriations near Ramallah that month; and an Israeli court ruling at the end of January that permitted Jews to pray at al-Haram al-Sharif in Jerusalem, the third holiest site in Islam and also the historical location of the Temple Mount. Additional protests were fueled by the arrests, fines and beatings that accompanied the demonstrations. And funeral processions for those who died in the strife turned into mass rallies. One activist later commented that "these were local and temporary slogans but they did indicate the people's indignation at the occupation and their desire to be rid of it." He noted that the public's growing political consciousness was evident in the broadening of the demands: the campaign against a particular settlement at Sebastia rapidly became a campaign against all Israeli settlements.[13] The wide range of political demands was reflected in a statement issued by the students of Bir Zeit University in March 1976: (1) stop all settlements, (2) stop desecrating Muslim and Christian holy places, (3) end all violence and provocation by soldiers, (4) release detainees, and (5) cancel the fines levied against students.

The apex of the civil strife was reached that March when Israeli soldiers stormed secondary schools in Nablus and Ramallah, and clubbed students in a dormitory at Bir Zeit University. They also broke into and damaged the municipality buildings in Hebron[14] and Beit Sahour, and clamped a ten day curfew on Ramallah and al-Bireh during which the Israeli press reported that "shots were fired into the air and any movement next to a window drew a volley of intimidation-fire."[15] Moreover, on March 17, 1976, Israeli settlers from Kiryat Arba entered neighboring Hebron. They fired warning shots at residents, beat and harassed people, and took three youths back to the settlement for further beatings and even attacks by dogs. The settlers forced a Muslim religious court judge to remove a barricade of stones that Arab youths had placed across a road. This indignity prompted the elderly mufti to state to an Israeli reporter: "I remembered a picture I once saw of how the Nazis forced religious Jews with beards to clean streets. I shall never forgive this blow. Never."[16] Later that month soldiers killed a child and several adults during demonstrations on the West Bank, and hundreds of people participated in the funeral processions, amidst cries of revenge.[17]

Earlier in March 1976 developments took a new turn when the Nablus municipality resigned in protest against the army's storming of a secondary school. This dramatic protest was duplicated by the municipalities of Ramallah, al-Bireh and Bir Zeit, which all resigned after a similar attack occurred at Bir Zeit University. The councils of Beit Sahour and (for a short period) Hebron followed suit, despite threats by Peres that Israeli military officers would be placed in charge of the towns.[18] The military also hoped that residents would turn against the former members of the municipalities in Ramallah and al-Bireh during the grueling ten day curfew. And they sought to weaken the nationalists by deporting to Lebanon two leading politicians from Hebron and al-Bireh who had declared their candidacies for municipal office.

Nevertheless, there was further mass civil disobedience on March 30, 1976, when general strikes were staged on the West Bank and Gaza. These were acts of solidarity with the Palestinians inside Israel, who were protesting land expropriations in Galilee. The Land Day (*Yawm al-Ard*) demonstrations were notable as the first concerted political action involving Arabs in Israel together with Arabs in the occupied territories. The common bond of Palestinian identity was reasserted and the deepset fear of further loss of land drew them together.

Municipal Council Elections

Politicians on the West Bank denounced Peres' self-rule plan and supported the civil disturbances that swept across the area during the winter of 1975–76. Nevertheless, they did not adopt a policy of total noncoöperation with the Israeli authorities. During that winter they devised a sophisticated strategy in response to Israel's announcement that municipal council elections would be held on the West Bank in April 1976. In the previous round of elections in 1972, many politicians had initially considered boycotting the poll, but had then decided to opt for the *status quo* and return the incumbents to power. This time, the National Front decided that its activists should gain control of the municipalities, taking influence away from the pro-Jordanian merchants and notables and preventing candidates handpicked by Israel from being elected. But they also asserted that controlling the municipalities would not derogate from their support for the PLO or serve as a step toward "self-rule."

The PNF stance was signalled by editorials in *al-Fajr* and *al-Shaʻb* in late November 1975. *Al-Shaʻb* maintained that the nationalists must participate in the elections in order to undermine the "traditional" leaders on the West Bank. *Al-Fajr*, in a heavily censored editorial, asserted that "we unhesitatingly support effective and open participation in the municipal elections," adding that the "right" people must participate and must agree on unified programs which oppose self rule and ensure that the municipalities not exceed their appointed functions.[19]

However, in late December 1975, the military governor of the West Bank announced that the voting qualifications would be changed so that women and propertyless men could vote. Those changes caused consternation among the nationalists. The mayors of Tulkarm, Nablus and Ramallah protested that the changes violated the Geneva Conventions by altering the *status quo* in the occupied territories, and they feared that accepting these changes would permit Israel to make other revisions in the laws. Some women's societies even considered boycotting the elections.[20] But the nationalists privately welcomed the broadened suffrage, since they could expect significant support from the newly enfranchised voters. Therefore, the PNF decided that it was more important to participate than to boycott. The Ramallah mayor announced that he would stand for reëlection, and other nationalists entered their names as well.[21] Nevertheless, they were criticized by pro-Jordanians for accepting the changes made by Israel in the Jordanian electoral law and, by supporters of the Popular Front, who opposed any coöperation with the occupying power.

The issue of contesting the elections also aroused controversy in Beirut. The Popular Front insisted that strikes, demonstrations and violence were the only valid forms of resistance to the occupation and that participating in the elections was an indication of how far the PLO had gone in abandoning the concept of a state comprising all of Palestine.[22] The PLO countered with the argument that the elections were really part of the Palestinians' resistance against the occupation: "elements will emerge in the municipal councils who are capable, with mass support, of standing up to the Zionist schemes."[23] And after the elections *Filastin al-Thawra* exclaimed:[24]

> There is no doubt that the decision of the nationalists to fight for the elections was a courageous step . . . [The election is] one of the greatest victories of the Palestinian revolution . . . the expulsion of the collaborators and reactionaries . . . and their replacement by nationalists, democrats and progressives within the framework of the nationalist lists supported by the PNF—the arm of PLO inside the occupied territories . . . The Palestinian revolution . . . has taken up a new weapon and a new position from which to direct mass struggle against Zionist occupation and the Jordanian régime.

The election campaign took place in the heightened atmosphere of demonstrations and strikes. It was punctuated by the resignations of many of the councils in March 1976 and the deportation of two candidates on March 27. National blocs were formed in each town with the slogan: "No to [Peres'] civil administration, Yes to the [Palestine] national front." Israel did not allow candidates to hold public rallies or to use overtly nationalist slogans (although posters tended to display the red, green, black and white colors of the Palestinian flag). Campaigning took place in informal gatherings in homes and clubs.

Seventy-two per cent of the 88,000 eligible voters (of whom 33,000 were women) went to the polls on April 12, 1976. Most people voted according to a mixture of criteria—political views, family ties and friendships—and the national blocs carefully blended these factors. In Ramallah, for example, a representative of each of the six most influential families appeared on the list, but they tended to be relatively young and well educated men, not the family elders. The list also included refugees from 1948 and Muslims in prominent positions, and a refugee clergyman became deputy mayor after the election. Similarly, in Nablus, the national bloc encompassed a wide range of candidates: a Ba'thist nationalist from a prominent family, Bassam Shak'a, who became mayor; the head of the Chamber of Commerce and a member of the dominant family, Thafer al-Masri, who became deputy mayor; a Communist and former administrative detainee, Khaldun 'Abd al-Haq; and an influential nationalist doctor, Hatem Abu Ghazaleh.

The elections resulted in a clean sweep for the national blocs in Hebron and Beit Jala, and strong majorities in Nablus, Ramallah, al-Bireh, Tulkarm, Beit Sahour, and Jericho. Karim Khalaf and Hilmi Hanun were reëlected in Ramallah and Tulkarm, respectively. The greatest upset occurred in Hebron where the young professionals in the national bloc defeated all of the followers of pro-Jordanian Shaykh Ja'bari. The Israeli-favored candidate in Ramallah, 'Abd al-Nur Jenho, not only lost his seat on the council but also came in last in the election, despite his strenuous efforts to buy support.[25] In Jericho and al-Bireh, the candidates who attracted the most votes represented the leftwing "progressive bloc" rather than the nationalist list, but in both cases ideologically neutral councilmen were selected to be mayors. Only in Bethlehem did the incumbent non-PNF mayor, Elias Freij, not only retain his seat but also command a majority of the council. And he demonstrated his political astuteness by selecting for deputy mayor the workers' representative and former detainee, George Hazboun.

An editorial in the Israeli newspaper *Davar* commented that the municipalities would now reflect more closely the feeling in the Arab "street", which was overwhelmingly pro-PLO and anti-Hussein.[26] Freij himself remarked that the new mayors and members of the councils were better educated, younger, and more outspoken: all support the PLO as their official representative; all state that they must not be an alternative to the PLO; all are dedicated to their cities and their functions as mayors; and all are sensitive to the current political trends on the West Bank, where the public has become increasingly united. If something happens in Hebron, he noted, it vibrates in Jenin and Nablus, too.[27]

The new mayors did not hesitate to express their views. Bassam Shak'a of Nablus stated succinctly: "The elections proved clearly that the Palestinians believe their sole legal representative to be the PLO."[28] Others commented that, even though they did not seek to become involved in political issues and would not challenge the right of the PLO to negotiate on their behalf, they often found themselves involved in political controversies. Daily life under occupation was inescapably political, and municipal projects inevitably had a political dimension.[29] The mayors of Beit Jala and al-Bireh had to react when the towns lost substantial lands to Israeli settlements; the Nablus municipality found itself in conflict with the military government when the government forbade the town from buying new electricity generators and tried to compel it to link into the Israeli electricity grid; and the Ramallah municipality contended with a threatened cut-off in water when it refused to accept water piped from Israel by the Israeli water authority. The nationalist municipalities resisted Israel's efforts to make the West Bank dependent on and permanently linked to its services and infrastructure. The politicization and constant dilemmas were stressed by Nablus councilman Hatem Abu Ghazaleh: "You can't talk about sewers to people who are sick and tired of living under occupation. What they want to hear is independence."[30]

NOTES, CHAPTER 4

1. Dani Rubinstein, *Davar*, November 16, 1975.
2. *Davar*, November 7, 1975.
3. Aziz Shehadeh, quoted in the *Jerusalem Post Magazine*, November 21, 1975, p. 11.
4. *Al-Fajr*, October 26, 1975.
5. *Al-Fajr*, October 28, 1975. See also the statements in *al-Fajr* on October 19, 25–30, and its editorial of October 26, 1975.
6. Statements by Dr. Haider 'Abd al-Shafei, President of the Red Crescent Society in Gaza, and the former mayor Raghib al-'Alami, *al-Fajr*, October 28, 1975.
7. *Al-Fajr* editorial, November 19, 1975.
8. *Al-Fajr* editorials, November 18 and 27, 1975, and *al-Quds* editorial, November 12, 1975.
9. *Al-Fajr*, December 27, 1975.
10. *Al-Watan*, January 1976 editorial, reprinted in *al-Ittihad*, January 27, 1976.
11. Numerous protests were made by the Nablus municipality and village leaders of Sebastia and Kaddum, with solidarity petitions sent from Tulkarm, Jenin, Ramallah, the Supreme Muslim Council in Jerusalem, and students at Bir Zeit and Bethlehem Universities. Demonstrations began on December 5, 1975: soldiers ordered away foreign newsmen while they kicked, clubbed and arrested demonstrators in Nablus. *International Herald Tribune* and *Guardian*, December 9, 1975; reports in *al-Fajr*, December 3 and 5, 1975.
12. Special assemblies were held in schools on January 12, 1976, the opening day of the UN debate. The debate was followed closely in the Arabic

press, and the US veto was denounced bitterly in the press (cf. *al-Fajr* editorial, January 28, 1976) and by the mayors of Bethlehem, Nablus and Tulkarm. Students staged strikes and attempted to demonstrate on January 27-28, 1976.

13. Dr. Ahmad Hamza Natshe in *Shu'un Filastiniyya*, May 1976.
14. Reported in *Yediot Ahronot*, March 24, 1976, and by Eric Silver in the *Guardian*, March 22, 1976: "The glass doors of the town hall, the water and electricity offices, and the adjoining Hebron museum, had all been shattered ... Chairs, desks and files were scattered to the wind. A telephone operator, Haj Ali Abu Snaineh, bared a swollen elbow and a bruised hip. He said he had been working at the switchboard when the soldiers rushed in. Shaykh Ja'bari's spokesman, Mr. Mukhlis Hammouri ... [said] 37 officials were hurt ... [and added:] People in England do not throw stones, because they are living in a democratic state. Here we live under military occupation and military rules. The only means to express our emotions and feelings against that occupation is by throwing stones against the army that violates the municipality, that violates the schools, that violates the mosque, and violates the houses. Had there been any other political or legal way to answer those challenges, we would have done that."
15. *Davar*, March 30, 1976. See also reports in the *Times* (London), March 9, 1976, on Nablus and the *Washington Star*, March 11, 1976, on Bir Zeit University.
16. Shaykh Rajab Bayad, quoted in *Yediot Ahronot*, March 24, 1976. Detailed reports on the March 17 actions in Hebron are contained in *al-Quds*, March 19, 1976; *Jerusalem Post*, March 18; *Yediot Ahronot*, March 18 and 24; *Times* (London), March 26 and 28; *Davar*, May 7; and *Ha'-Aretz*, May 6 and 16, 1976.
17. *Jerusalem Post*, March 22, 1976, and the *Guardian*, March 24, 1976. Dani Rubinstein deplored the "strong arm" policy of the military in *Davar*, March 30, 1976: "Beatings, slaps, curses and insults were daily and hourly occurrences over the past two weeks .... People were forced to stand against walls, take off their shoes, and sometimes even to remove tires from vehicles .... Nablus was quickly paralyzed, with people afraid to go out or to open shops—searches which everyone knew had only doubtful security value and whose sole aim was to harass and bother the residents."
18. *Al-Quds* and *Jerusalem Post*, March 17, 1976.
19. *Al-Sha'b*, November 29, 1975, and *al-Fajr*, November 23, 1975.
20. *Guardian*, January 5, 1976; *al-Fajr*, January 14 and 15, 1976.
21. *Guardian*, January 5, 1976; *al-Fajr*, January 6 and 25, 1976; *Davar*, January 27, 1976; and *Ha'Aretz*, January 26 and 28, 1976.
22. Bilal al-Hassan in *al-Safir*, March 6, 1976; also *al-Hadaf*, April 17 and May 8, 1976.
23. Mahmud Qadri in *al-Safir*, March 10, 1976.
24. *Filastin al-Thawra*, April 25, 1976.
25. *Ha'Aretz*, February 12, 1978.

26. *Davar*, April 16, 1976.
27. Interview with the author, May 13, 1976.
28. *HaOlam HaZeh*, May 12, 1976.
29. Bishara Daud, mayor of Beit Jala, in an interview with the author, May 13, 1976.
30. *Newsweek*, April 26, 1976, p. 25.

Chapter 5

INTERNAL AND EXTERNAL STRAINS

The civil disobedience movement and the municipal election campaign of 1975–76 were high points in the Palestinian struggle on the West Bank and Gaza. But the next year was deeply troubled. People experienced renewed feelings of powerlessness, pessimism over the prospects of Israeli withdrawal, and anxiety over the repercussions the sharp divisions in the Arab world held for the Palestinians. Morale was sapped by the civil war in Lebanon, the short-lived hope in October 1977 of gaining a Palestinian presence at Geneva, and the destabilizing and divisive impact of Sadat's peace initiative in November 1977. These setbacks were exacerbated by the election of Menachem Begin as Israel's prime minister in May 1977 and by the constant harassment of the new municipalities by the military government. Prospects for diplomatic gains seemed to have evaporated, and fears for the future of the West Bank and Gaza were magnified.

Inside the occupied territories, the mood remained tense during the summer and fall of 1976. The anniversary of Israel's independence on May 15, 1976, was marked by strikes and demonstrations that continued for several days in all the major towns. When a teenage girl was killed by soldiers in Nablus, 30,000 residents attended her funeral. Two Palestinian youths were shot to death by Israeli soldiers in Jerusalem, and a three-day curfew was imposed on Ramallah and al-Bireh on May 19. Extensive preventive arrests dampened the demonstrations on June 5, 1976, the ninth anniversary of the occupation. However, protests renewed in July and August when Israel imposed a new tax on the residents. Merchants argued that the Value Added Tax (VAT) was illegal according to the Geneva Conventions, since the pre-occupation tax structure was supposed to be maintained. They were also concerned about the VAT's potentially damaging effects on commerce, which was already suffering from escalating inflation. Merchants conducted widespread strikes that succeeded in forcing a few changes in Israeli tax policy. The government reduced the number of businesses affected by VAT and delayed the application of the tax outside East Jerusalem until December 1976.

During the summer of 1976, the atmosphere also remained volatile because Israeli settlers tried to add new colonies and militant Jews launched provocative actions in West Bank towns. Members of Gush Emunim attempted to found a colony near Jericho on August 2 and to conduct prayers on the Temple Mount in Jerusalem (al-Haram al-Sharif) three days later. Residents of Kiryat Arba also tried to gain control over some buildings in the center of Hebron and, in early October, they desecrated a Qur'an in Hebron's Ibrahim Mosque. The next day a large procession of Arab high school students marched to the mosque, where they clashed with Israeli soldiers and damaged the Jewish prayer area, including some Torah scrolls. In response, Kiryat Arba settlers set fire to a part of the mosque. Then the army clamped a two week curfew on the Arabs of Hebron. The inhabitants were penned indoors while Israelis were allowed to go to the mosque and the Jewish cemetery. Thousands of Israelis attended the "funeral" to bury the Torah scrolls desecrated by the Arab students.[1]

The atmosphere was ripe for demonstrations on Balfour Declaration Day (November 2, 1976). These demonstrations were met by heavy fines on participants and the expulsion of some students from school. Similarly, the business strikes over VAT that resumed in December 1976 were countered by scores of arrests and fines.[2] Palestinian residents were also disturbed by the army's confiscation of land near several towns, in particular at Gilo near Beit Jala and at Jabal Tawil, on the eastern edge of al-Bireh. Statements of solidarity with the threatened towns were sent from other municipalities and from the Jerusalem chamber of commerce. The deputy mayor of Nablus voiced the general concern:[3]

I condemn the confiscation of Arab lands, be it in Nablus, Ramallah or anywhere else. The continuous establishment of settlements on Arab lands is a grave danger to the inhabitants of the area.

The Palestinians' many grievances concerning the occupation were detailed and summarized in a petition that the mayors sent to the new American Secretary of State Cyrus Vance on January 31, 1977, on the eve of his first visit to Israel. The mayors stated that "our primary wish is to convey conditions of occupation ... without in any way wishing to assume a representative role for the Palestinian people, whose sole legitimate representative is the Palestine Liberation Organization." They then listed the problems the residents were facing, including religious and educational difficulties, land confiscation, and harsh prison conditions. A similar appeal to UN Secretary General Kurt Waldheim stressed Israeli violations of the UN charter and UN resolutions as well as the difficulties under occupation. It closed with an appeal for the implementation of the UN resolutions that call for Israeli withdrawal and "the establishment of the nucleus of an independent Palestinian state on this land."[4]

Repercussions from Inter-Arab Conflicts

The residents of the occupied territories were not only pressed by Israeli measures during 1976, but were also disturbed by inter-Arab conflicts that directly affected their fellow Palestinians and had repercussions on their own status and future. The most critical conflict occurred in Lebanon. The civil war that engulfed Lebanon in 1975–76 entered a particularly dangerous stage in June 1976 when Syria sent its troops into the country. Siding with right-wing Maronite militias against the left-wing forces and the PLO, the Syrian army allowed the rightists to besiege and destroy Tel Zaatar, a large Palestinian refugee camp in Beirut. The municipalities on the West Bank denounced the Syrian intervention and appealed to the Arab League to "stop the massacre" at Tel Zaatar. Residents sent blood, food and clothes to Lebanon.

Palestinian anger at the Syrian attack on the PLO was coupled with bitterness at the behavior of other Arab régimes that summer. The Kuwait government dissolved the National Assembly and clamped down on the press, as part of an apparent campaign to restrict Palestinian residents, who formed an active and articulate minority in Kuwait. Palestinians were even more angry at King Hussein, who briefly jailed about seventy prominent Palestinians in Amman after they sent a letter to the Syrian president deploring the intervention in Lebanon. Even that mildly-worded protest met with harsh restrictions, evidence of the continued submergence of the Palestinian majority on the East Bank. The Jerusalem press deplored the King's action and students demonstrated in Nablus to commemorate the sixth anniversary of the "black September" of 1970. These difficulties led Palestinians to feel hounded everywhere, their options increasingly restricted and no secure haven in sight. As difficulties mounted for Palestinians living in the Arab world, the need for a separate Palestinian state, even on a small portion of their historic territory, felt increasingly acute.

When the Arab rulers convened in Riyadh and Cairo in the autumn of 1976 to find a way to end the bloodshed in Lebanon, the mayors of the leading West Bank towns sent an urgent message. They condemned Syria, Jordan and the right-wing Lebanese groups and called on the Arab governments to "stand against the horrible conspiracy in Lebanon."[5] The mayor of Ramallah also sent a personal appeal, in which he asserted that the divisions in the Arab world and the rivalries among the Arab rulers were lengthening the occupation and threatening the future of the Palestinians. He argued that the states have moral duties to "shelter" the PLO and strive to end the occupation so that the Palestinians can be released from their "big prison" and the rest of the Palestinians can return home.[6]

The Arab summit conference, operating under Saudi pressure, did bring about a ceasefire in Lebanon which was policed by the Syrian army in the guise of an inter-Arab force. Palestinians felt a tremendous relief at the cessation of fighting, but the PLO leadership in Beirut found itself increasingly beholden to the Saudis. As a result, some PLO leaders began to maintain a distance from the more left-wing Palestinian groups in Beirut and in the occupied territories. The PLO's tactical move to the right caused tension within the municipal councils and within the editorial board of *al-Fajr* newspaper. Its editor, Bashir Barghuthi, was a leading Communist on the West Bank. *Al-Fajr*'s owner removed Barghuthi in November 1976. His dismissal was acquiesced in by all the members of the editorial board except Karim Khalaf, the mayor of Ramallah. Khalaf also deviated from the other mayors when he refused to sign a petition to US Secretary of State Cyrus Vance because it was not addressed simultaneously to the Soviet Foreign Minister, as co–convenor of the Geneva Conference. He even denounced the PLO-Jordan dialogue that was initiated by a meeting between King Hussein and Arafat in Cairo on March 8, 1977. But the other mayors viewed the meeting with cautious approval as a sign of eased tension and a possible harbinger of a future coördinated stand.

Although differences of emphasis and policy affected relationships among the municipalities and accelerated the disintegration of the National Front, the politicians were drawn together by pressures emanating from both Israel and Jordan. The Jordan government tried to make political support by the mayors a condition for the towns' receiving financial aid and even for Jordan's approval of the disbursement of funds that had been deposited in banks in Amman. Although the mayors of Gaza, Hebron, al-Bireh and Bethlehem trooped to Amman in the summer of 1976, the mayors of Nablus and Ramallah refused to go there to placate the King.[7] Amman even blocked the entry into the East Bank of mother-of-pearl products—the mainstay of Bethelehem's economy—for several months, alleging that the raw materials came from Israel and therefore importing them violated the Arab boycott of Israel. Bethlehem's mayor, Elias Freij, went as a supplicant to Amman, anxious to reopen the trade route as well as to obtain funding for his civic development plans.

Public resentment spread at this manipulation of financial aid, and the mayors began to discuss means to circumvent Amman by sending delegations directly to the oil-rich Arab states. They also wanted to find a way to undermine Israeli efforts to build up alternative leaders on the West Bank. The military government was instructing residents to obtain financial assistance, travel permits, family reunion certificates and other favors from such men as 'Abd al-Nur Jenho of Ramallah and Shaykh Muhammad 'Ali al-Ja'bari in Hebron, even though they had lost their municipal council seats in the elections in 1976.[8]

The effort to send municipal delegations to the Gulf states finally began in March 1977 when the Jericho municipality received a pledge of $250,000 from the ruler of Sharjah (United Arab Emirates).[9] The Arab League assigned an Arab city as a "twin" for each Palestinian town, from which the latter would obtain special funding for development projects. Ramallah was twinned with Algiers, for example, Jerusalem with Mecca, and Bir Zeit with Tunis. In the late spring of 1977 a half-dozen municipalities on the West Bank sent delegations to the Gulf and North Africa. Israeli officials soon expressed concern: the military administrators recognized that the fund raising would save Israel money, but they feared that "extensive development projects ... are also aimed at establishing a foundation for a Palestinian state" and therefore were wary of letting the funds enter the West Bank.[10]

In practice, control over the use of funds remained in the hands of both Israel and Jordan: Israel had to approve each project for which funds were raised, and Jordan had to allow the release of funds from the bank in Amman. Nevertheless, the publicity surrounding the fund raising and the fact that the money came from influential Arab régimes placed pressure on Jordan to approve requests and caused embarrassment for Israel when it rejected projects.

In addition to their concern about inter-Arab conflicts and pressures from Israel, politicians on the West Bank and Gaza were anxious about the decisions that might be adopted at the thirteenth session of the Palestine National Council. The PNC met in Cairo in March 1977, after several delays. The last PNC, held in June 1974, had adopted critically important decisions, such as the acceptance of a political "entity" once the occupation would end, and support for the PLO to pursue a diplomatic route as well as conduct a military struggle.

Since 1974, the PLO's fortunes had plunged from the high

point of its recognition by the UN and the nationalist sweep of the West Bank municipal elections to the low point of the civil war in Lebanon in 1975–76. Just as the West Bank politicians had pressed the PLO in 1974–75 to adopt a realistic policy and spell out its specific political and territorial aims, politicians now wanted the PLO, at the PNC in 1977, to consolidate its diplomatic gains and call publicly for a separate state on the West Bank and the Gaza Strip. A few even wanted the PLO Covenant revised, but most viewed this as unlikely and premature.

Since the Israeli military government prevented residents of the occupied territories from attending the PNC, their views could only be expressed in petitions and editorials. One editorial in *al-Quds*, for example, called the PNC the Palestinian "parliament-in-exile" and urged its delegates to distinguish between their long-term "vision" and the "phases" needed to realize that vision. It suggested "as a starting point . . . the proposed Palestinian state on the West Bank and the Gaza Strip, special relations with Jordan, and coöperation with peace negotiations."[11] A long analysis in *al-Fajr* also stressed that Palestinian aims must be stated "in accordance with an earthly time-span" and argued that the PNC should grant the PLO leadership "the freedom to decide whether to participate in the Geneva conference."[12] A memorandum from all 24 West Bank mayors was read at the PNC as well as a petition with 7,000 signatures that called for Arab unity, Israeli withdrawal from the territories occupied in 1967, an independent state in those territories, and the return of the Palestinian refugees.[13]

The 1977 PNC upheld the decisions of the 1974 council to attempt the diplomatic route and accept a limited settlement, despite strong and vocal criticism from "rejectionist" delegates. The PNC even endorsed the idea of establishing a "state" (rather than an "entity") in the territories occupied by Israel and empowered the PLO leadership to enter into negotiations. Some West Bankers were disappointed with the PNC, since it did not launch any new diplomatic initiative. But the politicians accepted the results in public, stating that the political circumstances did not permit the PNC to go any further.[14]

Despite the weakness of the PLO and the divisions inside it, Palestinians in the occupied territories and elsewhere continued to view it as the embodiment of their national aspirations and the one organization that would work for their interests as Palestinians. Moreover, identification with the political structure that represented the entire Palestinian community helped to strengthen the morale and reduce the sense of isolation among those living under occupation.

The Israeli Elections

The 1977 Israeli election campaign was watched closely by the Palestinians. Some argued that there was little difference between the Likud and Labor parties, since both would increase settlements in the occupied territories.[15] But most people saw distinctions between the two leading parties and held a greater animosity toward Menachem Begin, the preëminent leader of the Likud.

Begin's party won the elections on May 17, 1977, and he promptly visited the settlement of Kaddum, which had been established by the Gush Emunim movement in defiance of the Labor government. There he proclaimed that all of the West Bank was "liberated" territory. Begin's assertion triggered fear, panic and then anger on the West Bank. *Al-Quds* editorialized: "We wish to emphasize to Mr. Begin that we live here in our country and homeland, and we are no less determined to keep our lands than Begin is determined to uproot us." And the Jericho mayor articulated the general fears:[16]

We are apprehensive and worried because the situation has now become very perilous, and tension will rise. The danger is that Begin has already crystallized his views on the Palestinians and opposes any sort of agreement which would lead to fulfillment of the just demands of the Palestinians.

The mayor of Hebron feared a "hot summer" with more troubles over settlements and religious claims, particularly as relations with the military government and Israeli settlers were already tense.[17] In fact, the Israeli government persisted in harassing the municipalities and searching for alternative leaders on the West Bank. A member of the Nablus municipality voiced the widespread complaint that the military government was trying to paralyze development activity: no building of schools, no enlargement of the electricity plant, and no foreign aid to the town.[18] The military authorities also kept trying to take authority away from the elected mayors and encouraged other "notables" to supersede them. The Ramallah military governor, for example, named the repudiated politician 'Abd al-Nur Jenho as its representative for citizens' demands. Jenho participated in the military government's deliberations on linking Ramallah to the Israeli water system, a measure which the mayor, Karim Khalaf, resisted until the Israelis threatened to cut off the water supply and he had to capitulate.[19] In Hebron, the military authorities encouraged the former Jordanian minister Mustafa Doudin to support the return of the West Bank to Jordan, and they were pleased when Burhan Ja'bari, a son of the former mayor, called for self-determination for the people living in the territories without establishing any link to the PLO.[20] Meanwhile, the military urged residents to turn to Doudin and Ja'bari for assistance and special favors, bypassing the mayor, Fahd Qawasmah.

The most bizarre campaign focused on Hussein Shuyukhi, a little-known lawyer from Hebron. Shuyukhi headed a delegation to Amman in early August 1977, where he apparently asserted that he could organize support on the West Bank for its return to Jordan. He then declared that he would form a pro-Jordanian political party and would hold a meeting of Palestinians who opposed the PLO. But he cancelled the press conference that he had scheduled to announce his supporters, and the leading adherents of King Hussein dismissed Shuyukhi contemptuously.[21]

Nevertheless, the publicity surrounding Shuyukhi embarrassed the pro-Jordanian politicians. His initiative came at a delicate juncture and was particularly awkward for the leaders who sought a course that would accommodate US and Jordanian interests. On August 10, 1977, four political figures had broken the boycott called by the mayors and met with US Secretary of State Cyrus Vance in Foreign Minister Moshe Dayan's home outside Tel Aviv. They presented Vance with a petition that supported the concept of an interim period before the establishment of a Palestinian state on the West Bank and Gaza. During that period a neutral "peace-promoting force" would ensure security and supervise a plebiscite. Once established, the state would coexist with Israel on the basis of mutual recognition, nonaggression, open borders, economic and cultural exchanges, and shared sovereignty over Jerusalem.[22]

The mayors, who all boycotted the meeting, issued their own statement. That manifesto also asserted the Palestinians' right to establish an independent state, but it affirmed that the PLO was the sole representative of the Palestinians and that no other individuals could legitimately promote themselves as alternative spokesmen.[23] In fact, the nationalist politicians tended to be more critical of the four men for breaking ranks than for the content of their proposal. As a result of the Shuyukhi initiative, the criticism by the nationalist mayors, and public statements by Israeli ministers that they would support any Palestinians who opposed the PLO,[24] the four conservative figures backed away from their initiative and hastened to reaffirm their support for the PLO.[25]

By mid-September 1977, the period of publicly-expressed divisions had ended. When petitions were sent to the UN for the opening of the General Assembly session, all the West Bank mayors, members of most of the chambers of commerce, and leaders of social organizations, unions, religious, youth and women's societies joined in demanding Israeli withdrawal and affirming the Palestinians' right to an independent state under the PLO. Similarly, in the Gaza Strip the conservative mayors of Gaza and Khan Yunis signed another petition together with the strongly nationalist members of the Gaza Red Crescent Society.[26]

But some confusion was caused by the rumor that residents of the West Bank and Gaza might be included in a Palestinian negotiating team at Geneva. When the proposition was first raised in early October 1977, the politicians were uncertain how to respond. Several mayors stated that no one living under Israeli occupation could negotiate effectively or credibly with Israel.[27] Al-Sha'b newspaper, published in East Jerusalem, even denounced the idea as a "conspiracy to deprive the Palestinians of the right to choose their own representatives."[28] Later that month, when it became apparent that the PLO might accept the formula and the names of possible delegates were rumored, criticism began to die down.[29] A few mayors even stated that they would join a delegation if the PLO authorized them. But this was a short-lived prospect. Just as the public began to hope that comprehensive negotiations might open in Geneva, Sadat's precipitous visit to Jerusalem sowed confusion and consternation.

The Sadat Initiative

Palestinian reactions to Sadat's diplomatic initiative must be considered in three contexts: first, the reactions to Sadat's expressed aims, notably the hopes raised by his speech at the Knesset, and the concern resulting from his subsequent bilateral negotiations; second, official Israeli responses to Sadat, indicated by Begin's limited self-rule plan and the continued restrictive policies in the occupied territories; and third, the resulting polarization in the Arab world and the difficulties faced by the Arab states that sought to develop alternatives to Sadat's strategy.

Sadat's announcement that he would visit Jerusalem in November 1977 immediately provoked hostile demonstrations on the West Bank, because residents feared that he would sign a separate peace treaty with Israel and because they objected to his visiting Jerusalem while its Arab residents still suffered from occupation. When Sadat attended prayers at al-Aqsa mosque, the religious judge called on Sadat to "listen to the voice of al-Aqsa, the voice of Palestine in mourning." And people shouted as Sadat left the mosque, "Remember Palestine, oh Sadat!"[30] Despite their criticisms, several prominent residents met with him at his hotel and the mayor of Qalqilya voiced a widespread viewpoint: "If this trip results in the attainment of the legitimate rights of the Palestinian people and the establishment of the Palestinian state, we welcome it."[31] Some noted that Sadat's visit meant that Israelis could no longer claim that Arabs would never accept Israel's existence. Others commented that the trip placed Israel in an embarrassing situation, since Israel would now have to state whether it would relinquish territories in return for peace. The ambivalent responses turned

to expressions of relief when Sadat delivered a states-
manlike address at the Knesset in which he strongly affirmed the need for Palestinian self-determination. Even so,
some were suspicious of his failure to mention the PLO explicitly. The mayor of Hebron remarked:[32]

At first, we rejected Sadat's initiative. We were afraid
that Sadat would give many things away, things that be-
longed to the Palestinians. But his speech to the Israeli
Knesset was good. The only bad thing was that he left out
the PLO. If this means he is trying to eliminate the PLO
from the problem, we don't agree.

Political activists tended to support Sadat's statements
and his courage in challenging Israel to negotiate a comprehensive peace treaty. But they realized that Sadat's trip
had to be judged by its results. The Halhul mayor noted:
"People here want what President Sadat is preaching, but
they don't believe Israel [will] give it."[33] There were also politicians who questioned Sadat's intentions. When he sought
to woo Palestinians away from the PLO by encouraging separate delegations to Cairo in December 1977, a large gathering at the Arab Graduates Club in Jerusalem voiced its support for the PLO and opposition to such delegations, although it also praised the Egyptians for their past sacrifices
on behalf of the Palestinian cause.[34] Delegations went to
Cairo from Hebron and Gaza, but the more prominent figures canceled plans to go there. One leading resident from
Jerusalem remarked that it would be appropriate to send a
delegation after the negotiations achieved results, but not
before.[35]

Suspicions that Israel would not reciprocate Sadat's initiative were underscored by Begin's self-rule plan. Moreover, the negotiations in Cairo, Ismailiyya and Jerusalem in
December 1977 and January 1978 were strictly bilateral, and

therefore renewed fears that Sadat would conclude a separate agreement and that he lacked enough bargaining power and diplomatic skill to wrest serious concessions from Israel. One editor called the negotiations a "cover" for a separate treaty.[36]

Israel's response to Sadat elicited bitter reactions from Palestinians. Although Sadat, in his Knesset speech, had expressed a comprehension of the deep-seated Jewish trauma, Begin, in his response, showed no comparable understanding of Arab fears or the Palestinian trauma. The Begin plan caricatured their aspirations for self-government. Elias Freij, mayor of Bethlehem, reacted angrily: "We have known for years that Israel would not give up the territory and the Sadat initiative has forced them to unmask their cruel intentions."[37]

Moreover, the day-to-day practices of the Israeli military government remained unchanged. Several members of municipal councils in Jericho, el-Bireh and Beit Jala faced trial in the winter and spring of 1978 on charges of assaulting Israeli policemen.[38] The Israelis even dissolved three village councils, replacing the members with their hand-picked officials, and they dismissed the Beit Jala mayor in July 1978.[39] The restrictions reached a point of absurdity when the military governor refused to let the mayor of Jericho hold a banquet for his fellow mayors after he returned from a fund-raising trip abroad.[40] That particular ban was eased in June, when the governor permitted mayors to meet to discuss municipal, but not political, matters.[41]

One notable change did occur in May 1978, when Defense Minister Ezer Weizman fired the military governor of the West Bank for his role in covering up some soldiers' brutal behavior against school children in Beit Jala on March 21, 1978.[42] Weizman then released an outspoken Palestinian journalist who had been detained without charge for six weeks,[43] allowed the Nablus municipality to purchase three electricity generators,[44] and let a popular politician return from exile.[45] Weizman also opposed Agriculture Minister Ariel Sharon when he instigated the Israel Land Authority's refusal to let Arabs who live abroad grant powers-of-attorney over their property to relatives remaining on the West Bank.[46]

However, Weizman's policy was set firmly in the context of the Begin self-rule plan, which would include giving the municipalities more autonomy and placing Arabs in key posts in departments in the territories.[47] He assumed that "we are two peoples [who] are destined to live together in this country and we have to find the means ... [to] co-exist."[48] He also strongly supported the establishment of six urban settlements near heavily populated areas on the West Bank. Thus his policies were designed to hasten the integration of the West Bank into Israel and to mute Arab criticism. However, the residents still felt that they were living under alien and arbitrary rule: Israel might allow one deportee to return, but not others; and one municipality might acquire an electricity generator, but another might be denied a similar project, according to the whim of the military governor and the Minister of Defense. "We feel like characters in a novel by Franz Kafka," one councilman complained.[49]

The third context for understanding Palestinian reactions to Sadat's initiative involved inter-Arab relations. West Bank and Gaza politicians felt that they required a united Arab front in order to gain significant diplomatic leverage over Israel. Sadat broke that front and forced the PLO into greater dependence on Syria. The politicians were also concerned because the "steadfastness front" that sought to counter Sadat seemed unable to formulate a viable diplomatic alternative to Sadat's bold move. Iraq and Libya remained more "rejectionist" than Syria and the PLO, and Saudi Arabia and Jordan tried to maintain their neutrality.

West Bank residents did demonstrate support for the Arab summit meeting in Tripoli, Libya, in December 1977 and the Algiers summit in February 1978,[50] but many were skeptical of relying on any Arab leaders. One left-wing Palestinian politician leveled his criticism at all the régimes: "The memories of Jordan in 1970 and Lebanon in 1976 are still fresh ... We have learned that the help given by the leaders of the Arab states is limited and goes only up to a point."[51] Their suspicions seemed justified when no Arab state assisted the PLO against the Israeli invasion of South Lebanon in March 1978, launched after the guerrilla attack near Tel Aviv, in which 34 Israelis were killed. Palestinians called the fighting in Lebanon the second "battle of Karameh." One Nablus politician asserted: "The PLO won support from West Bankers by standing alone in Lebanon against Israel for seven or eight days, longer than all the Arab countries did in the Six-Day War."[52] Demonstrations swept the West Bank and even spread to Gaza, where 300 youths were arrested. But most politicians realized that the Palestinians needed Arab support and could not afford a major rift with those régimes.[53]

By the summer of 1978, residents expected the worst from the Israeli government, were apprehensive that Sadat was moving down the road to a separate treaty, and feared that the Palestinians were vulnerable in the rest of the Arab world. Faced with these pressures and this sense of isolation, the politicians drew together. They recognized that the Palestinians would weaken themselves if they emphasized internal ideological differences. Some discussed reviving the National Front, which had become moribund after the municipal council elections in 1976.[54] But most people were simply holding tight. On the one hand they tried to maintain the semblance of a normal life, by strengthening their educational system and drawing up blueprints for hospitals and housing projects. On the other hand, they expected that the September 1978 trilateral negotiations at Camp David would fail and Sadat would have to return to the Arab fold, resuming the agonizingly slow process toward a comprehensive settlement.

NOTES, CHAPTER 5

1. Eyewitness report, including interview with Fahd Qawasmah, mayor of Hebron, October 6, 1976.
2. *Davar*, December 12, 1976; *Yediot Ahronot*, December 15, 1976.
3. *Al-Sha'b*, September 3, 1976.
4. The petition to Vance was written in English. Initiated by the mayors of Nablus, Hebron and Halhul, it was not signed by the mayors of Bethlehem or Ramallah. The petition to Waldheim was written in Arabic and was signed by the mayor of Ramallah as well as the other important mayors.
5. Sent September 29, 1976, by the mayors of Nablus, Hebron, Ramallah, al-Bireh, and Qalqilya.
6. Karim Khalaf's letter, printed in *al-Sha'b*, October 26, 1976.
7. *Ha'Aretz*, November 23, 1976.
8. Jenho was completely beholden to the Israeli military government. After his defeat in the election, he killed a member of the Liftawi family (apparently for a combination of political and gambling-debt motives), but he was acquitted by a special Israeli military court. He received some protection from the army and was licensed to carry a gun.
9. Israel radio broadcast, March 24, 1977.
10. Israel radio broadcast, May 26, 1977.
11. *Al-Quds*, March 12, 1977.
12. *Al-Fajr*, March 9, 1977, analysis by the political editor, Ghassan Tahbub. He also urged the PLO to encourage Palestinian dialogue with Israeli peace groups, even though they were weak in the Israeli political arena.
13. Reported in the Foreign Broadcast Information Service (FBIS), *Middle East and North Africa*, March 16, 1977, p. A7.
14. Only Elias Freij criticized the PNC in public (Israel radio broadcast, March 22, 1977). The differing reactions to US President Jimmy Carter's off-hand reference to the Palestinians' right to a "homeland" should also be noted. Khalaf derided the statement as merely "throwing dust in the eyes of the Arab leaders," whereas Qawasmah echoed the hope of many people that it was "a first step on the way towards the recognition by the USA of the rights of the Palestinians" and therefore was "an important declaration." Both mayors were quoted in *L'Orient-Le Jour* (Beirut), March 19, 1977.
15. For example, editorial in *al-Sha'b*, January 9, 1977.
16. Quoted in the *Jerusalem Post*, May 19, 1977.
17. *Ha'Aretz*, March 22, 1977, analyzed the troubles between the military and the mayors. There were also confrontations in April and May 1977 over settlements: the Gush Emunim march to Mes'ha on April 5 and the establishment of a colony there on May 1 had caused demonstrations in Nablus from April 6 to 13 and May 3–7. Two people were killed

by Israeli soldiers in demonstrations in Qabatiyya village, north of Nablus, on May 3. The demonstrations were provoked by reports that a settlement would be founded nearby. There was also the mysterious night-time harassment of the village of Deir Abu Mash'al, West of Ramallah, during late April and May 1977.

18. Dr. Hatem Abu Ghazaleh, quoted in *Ha'Aretz*, July 17, 1977. Also complaints by the mayor of Nablus, quoted in *Ha'Aretz*, August 3, 1977.

19. *Zu HaDerech*, September 7 and 20, 1977.

20. *The New York Times*, August 11, 1977; *Davar*, September 11, 1977.

21. On Shuyukhi's efforts, see *Davar*, August 22, 1977 and *The Christian Science Monitor*, August 24, 1977. *Ma'ariv*, August 22, 1977, quoted criticisms of Shuyukhi by Elias Freij, mayor of Bethlehem, and the staunchly pro-Jordanian editor of *al-Quds*, Mahmud Abu Zuluf. Abu Zuluf stated: "[It's] an initiative that is not serious and will lead to nothing and that does not deserve all this interest."

22. The four were Aziz Shehadeh (Ramallah lawyer), Burhan Ja'bari (Hebron), Mustafa Doudin (Hebron), and Judge Nihad Jarallah (Jerusalem). *The New York Times*, August 11, 1977; *Davar*, August 11, 1977; *Jerusalem Post* international edition, August 16, 1977.

23. The mayors' statement was addressed (at Khalaf's insistence) to both Vance and Gromyko, as the co-chairmen of the Geneva conference. Translated from *al-Fajr* in FBIS, *Middle East and North Africa*, August 16, 1977. Signed by the mayors of Ramallah, al-Bireh, Nablus, Hebron, Halhul, Qalqilya, Tulkarm, Beitunya and Dura, and the deputy mayor of Bethlehem.

24. For example, the statement by Defense Minister Ezer Weizman quoted in *Yediot Ahronot*, September 5, 1977.

25. For example, the statement by Aziz Shehadeh quoted in *Ma'ariv*, August 22, 1977; also *al-Hamishmar*, September 18, 1977. These politicians were also embarrassed by Begin's statement on August 14, 1977, that services on the West Bank and Gaza would be "equalized" with those in Israel, since this hinted at annexation. Shehadeh, Anwar Nusseibeh and Rashad Shawwa protested, and Fahd Qawasmah of Hebron noted that the towns could use more schools and hospitals but "if it's a political thing, we will refuse to be a part of it." *The New York Times*, August 16, 1977.

26. The West Bank petition was signed by 66 people, including the mayors of Ramallah, al-Bireh, Nablus, Jericho, Beit Jala, Beit Sahour, Bethlehem, Tulkarm, Hebron, Halhul and Dura. The Gaza petition was signed by (among others) the mayor of Gaza, Rashad Shawwa; the mayor of Khan Yunis, Sulaiman al-Astal; the director general of the Health Ministry in the Gaza Strip, Dr. Khair Abu Ramadan; the president of the Red Crescent Society, Dr. Haider 'Abd al-Shafei; the head of the women's society, Miss Yusra Barbari; the head of the lawyers' society, Fayez Abu Rahmeh; and the principal of Gaza College, Dr. Wadi' Tarazi. UN Document A/32/313, October 27, 1977; *Davar*, October 20, 1977; advertisement in *The New York Times*, December 16, 1977.

27. Karim Khalaf stated: "If we [mayors] went to Geneva we would get local autonomy. If Arafat goes, he will get a state." Quoted in *The Christian Science Monitor*, December 14, 1977. Bassam Shak'a added: "the one who is living under occupation is not authorized to negotiate with the conqueror." Quoted in *Zu HaDerech*, November 30, 1977.
28. Quoted in *The Christian Science Monitor*, October 13, 1977.
29. *The New York Times*, October 25, 1977. Acceptable names included the mayors of Nablus, Ramallah, Tulkarm, Hebron, al-Bireh and Jericho, but not the mayors of Bethlehem or Gaza.
30. *Jerusalem Post* international edition, November 23, 1977.
31. Shaykh Ja'bari was the only West Banker to meet Sadat at the airport. The group that met with him on November 21, 1977, in Jerusalem included Anwar Khatib, Hikmat al-Masri, Rashad Shawwa, Elias Freij, Mustafa Doudin, Judge Nihad Jarallah, the mayor of Deir al-Balah Sulaiman al-Faranjah, Ibrahim Abu Sittah of Gaza, Naim 'Abd al-Hadi, and Shaykh Fara Mussader of Nusseirat refugee camp in Gaza.
32. Fahd Qawasmah, quoted in *The Christian Science Monitor*, November 29, 1977. *Al-Nahar* (Beirut), November 22, 1977, reported praise for Sadat's speech in *al-Quds* and *al-Sha'b*.
33. Muhammad Hasan Milhem, quoted in *The Christian Science Monitor*, December 14, 1977; also in *CSM*, November 29, 1977.
34. Statement signed by eleven mayors, three deputy mayors, and the heads of several professional and charitable societies; *Ha'Aretz*, December 20, 1977 and *Journal of Palestine Studies*, number 27, spring 1977, pp. 195–6. Sadat's campaign against Palestinians, launched after the murder of Egyptian journalist Yusef Sibai on Cyprus, was decried in editorials in *al-Fajr*, February 20 and 28, 1978.
35. The head of the chamber of commerce, Fayek Barakat, quoted in *In These Times* (Chicago), January 11–17, 1978. Shaykh Hashem Khuzundar of Gaza headed a delegation to Ismailiyya (*Jerusalem Post* international edition, December 20, 1977) and Mustafa Doudin and Burhan Ja'bari led one from Hebron. But 'Abd al-Ra'uf Faris of Nablus cancelled plans for a delegation (*Ma'ariv*, December 30, 1977) and many people withdrew from the Gaza delegation when they realized that participating would be interpreted as an anti-PLO action. Weizman publicly backed the delegations (Israel TV, November 24, 1977) and personnel in the military government telephoned many politicians urging them to participate. Freij published a denial of any intent to visit Cairo in *al-Fajr*, December 9, 1977, and the municipalities of Ramallah, al-Bireh, Beni Zaid, Beitunya and Silwad placed an "important announcement" in *al-Fajr* on December 23, 1977, in which they stated that "all who participate in the delegation to Egypt represent only themselves" and reaffirmed that the PLO is the sole legitimate representative of the Palestinians.
36. Ma'mun al-Sayyed, editor of *al-Fajr*, quoted in *Events* (London), December 16, 1977. See also editorials in *al-Fajr* on January 17, 20, 25, and February 3, 1978.

37. Quoted in *Time*, March 27, 1978.
38. The trial of the mayor of Beit Jala, Bishara Daud, and three councilmen began in mid-December 1977 (*al-Fajr*, December 8, 1977). Dr. Azmi Shu'aibi of al-Bireh was put on trial February 1, 1978, for allegedly assaulting an Israeli border police officer and instigating people to demonstrate, eleven months previously (*al-Fajr*, January 31, 1978). And Yusif 'Ali Murar of Jericho was tried for allegedly punching a police sergeant while inciting pupils to demonstrate (*Ma'ariv*, March 19, 1978). Jad Mikhail of Ramallah was detained for seven weeks in the autumn, but was released without any charges being pressed (Reuter, September 4, 1978; Israel radio broadcast, October 21, 1978).
39. *Al-Fajr*, April 21, 1978, report on Deir Dubwan. The councils in Yatta and Qabatiyya were also dissolved. The sentencing and dismissal of Bishara Daud and the other three Beit Jala councilmen was protested by the West Bank mayors in a manifesto on July 4, 1978. They also appealed, unsuccessfully, to the Israeli high court against the dismissals. *Ha'Aretz*, July 5, 1978; *Yediot Ahronot*, July 6, 1978; *al-Fajr*, July 6 and 7, 1978.
40. Israel radio broadcast, May 4, 1978. The mayor of Qalqilya also stated that the military governor had forbidden him from holding political meetings with other mayors; *al-Fajr*, May 5, 1978. The mayors' fund-raising trips were quite successful: Shak'a, for example, returned with pledges totalling over $11 million and Khalaf with $10 million.
41. *Jerusalem Post* international edition, June 20, 1978; military governor statement to Hilmi Hanun, mayor of Tulkarm, *al-Fajr*, June 14, 1978.
42. An interview with a young soldier who participated in the attack on the Askandar Khuri school, in which he expressed his shock and shame at the teargassing, was printed in *Ma'ariv*, September 4, 1978.
43. Raymonda Tawil of Ramallah. *Jerusalem Post*, May 8, 1978.
44. Israel radio broadcast, June 20, 1978.
45. Dr. Ahmad Hamza Natshe, who had been deported in March 1976, returned to Hebron on June 26, 1978. *Al-Fajr*, June 26 and 27, 1978.
46. Arab protests were led by Elias Freij and Aziz Shehadeh. *Ma'ariv*, May 23, 1978; *Jerusalem Post*, May 25, 1978.
47. *Al-Fajr*, May 25, 1978.
48. Israel radio broadcast, June 20, 1978; Dani Rubinstein's analysis of Weizman's policy, *Davar*, July 7, 1978.
49. Deputy mayor of Ramallah, Rev. Awdeh Rantisi, quoted in *The Christian Science Monitor*, May 23, 1978.
50. *Al-Fajr*, December 4, 1977, and February 6–9, 1978.
51. Bashir Barghuthi, quoted in *Zu HaDerech*, November 30, 1977.
52. Hatem Abu Ghazaleh, Nablus councilman, quoted in *The New York Times*, March 24, 1978; see also Freij, quoted in *Yediot Ahronot*, March 16, 1978; *Al-Sha'b* editorial, quoted in *Davar*, March 24, 1978; and *The Christian Science Monitor*, March 28, 1978.
53. For example, editorial in *al-Fajr*, March 23, 1978.
54. Editorial by Bashir Barghuthi in *al-Tali'ah*, August 31, 1978.

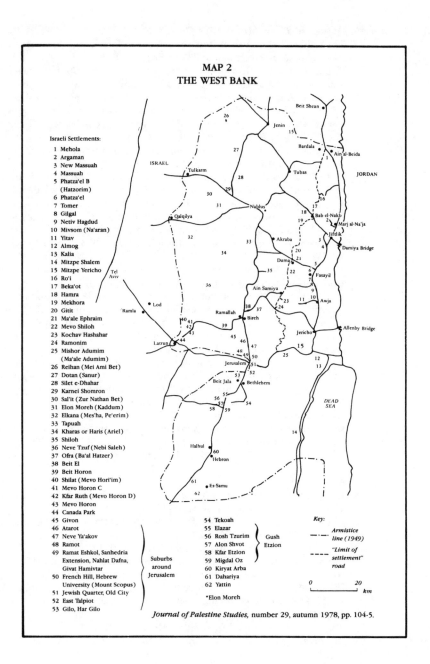

MAP 2
THE WEST BANK

Israeli Settlements:

1 Mehola
2 Argaman
3 New Massuah
4 Massuah
5 Phatza'el B
  (Hatzorim)
6 Phatza'el
7 Tomer
8 Gilgal
9 Netiv Hagdud
10 Mivsom (Na'aran)
11 Yitav
12 Almog
13 Kalia
14 Mitzpe Shalem
15 Mitzpe Yericho
16 Ro'i
17 Beka'ot
18 Hamra
19 Mekhora
20 Gitit
21 Ma'ale Ephraim
22 Mevo Shiloh
23 Kochav Hashahar
24 Ramonim
25 Mishor Adumim
  (Ma'ale Adumim)
26 Reihan (Mei Ami Bet)
27 Dotan (Sanur)
28 Silet e-Dhahar
29 Karnei Shomron
30 Sal'it (Zur Nathan Bet)
31 Elon Moreh (Kaddum)
32 Elkana (Mes'ha, Pe'erim)
33 Tapuah
34 Kharas or Haris (Ariel)
35 Shiloh
36 Neve Tzuf (Nebi Saleh)
37 Ofra (Ba'al Hatzer)
38 Beit El
39 Beit Horon
40 Shilat (Mevo Hori'im)
41 Mevo Horon C
42 Kfar Ruth (Mevo Horon D)
43 Mevo Horon
44 Canada Park
45 Givon
46 Atarot
47 Neve Ya'akov
48 Ramot
49 Ramat Eshkol, Sanhedria
  Extension, Nahlat Dafna,
  Givat Hamivtar
50 French Hill, Hebrew
  University (Mount Scopus)
51 Jewish Quarter, Old City
52 East Talpiot
53 Gilo, Har Gilo

54 Tekoah
55 Elazar
56 Rosh Tzurim
57 Alon Shvot
58 Kfar Etzion
59 Migdal Oz
60 Kiryat Arba
61 Dahariya
62 Yattin

*Elon Moreh

Suburbs
around
Jerusalem

Gush
Etzion

Key:

–·–·– Armistice
line (1949)

– – – "Limit of
settlement"
road

0   20
|————————| km

Journal of Palestine Studies, number 29, autumn 1978, pp. 104-5.

Chapter 6

EPILOGUE

The previous chapters have traced the reëmergence of a strong and well articulated Palestinian national identity among the Arabs on the West Bank and the Gaza Strip over the past thirteen years, and have described their efforts to institutionalize and express that identity. The Arab residents have been hampered in their attempts to strengthen their social and political institutions by the policies of the Israeli military government. Israel has also prevented them from linking their local structures to the central political institutions of the Palestinian national movement, headquartered in Beirut. And their relations with Jordan and Egypt, former ruling powers, have frequently been acrimonious.

The residents have been buffeted by external crises: the shock of the occupation in 1967, the failure of the guerrilla movement to liberate them from Israeli rule in the late 1960s, the rout of the PLO in Jordan in 1970, and the debilitating civil war in Lebanon in the mid-70s. Hopes were raised by the October War and the PLO's diplomatic successes in 1974, but were dashed by the slow pace of negotiations and Israel's success in gaining a separate peace with Egypt in 1979. The Palestinian residents hope that negotiations will alleviate their situation and release them from occupation, but they often fear that only force will compel Israel to relinquish its grip on the territories.

The Effects of Occupation

The Israeli occupation has affected the Palestinians in both tangible and intangible ways. The most important tangible impact has been on economic life and land holdings. The West Bank and the Gaza Strip have become heavily dependent on Israel for trade and employment. There is a dearth of job opportunities for educated people in the territories, and industry has stagnated. The staggering rate of inflation in Israel in recent years has caused serious hardship in the territories. The extent to which these trends represent the creation of a long term dependence on Israel remains a matter of debate. Credible economists have argued that the process is reversible once the occupation ends and the Palestinians gain control over their economic life.[1]

The establishment of Israeli settlements on the West Bank and the Gaza Strip, the seizure of water resources, and the attachment of the territories' electricity and telephone networks to the Israeli systems are further changes that link the territories materially to Israel. In particular, the creation of more than seventy settlements and the appropriation of nearly a third of the land make it difficult for Palestinians to imagine the Israeli government ever agreeing to relinquish the territories. Rather, the settlements bind the West Bank and Gaza tighter to Israel.[2]

The tangible effects are readily visible. The intangible effects are less apparent, but no less real or important. The thirteen years of occupation have had a major impact on Palestinian attitudes and perceptions. Palestinians have come to see the Israelis as a people and as individuals. They sometimes have business dealings with Israelis, and have made a few friendships. But they have also experienced the weight of Israeli power, which dominates their daily lives and constricts their options for the future. Moreover, they experience the all-pervasive tension of occupation, from which none can escape. The novelist Sahar Khalifah used the word "tension" to epitomize life under occupation:[3]

> Tension inside, tension outside. . . . You feel you are in a
> whirlpool, a whirlwind, a pressure cooker. . . . Occupation,
> demonstrations, news, trials, prisons, demolished houses,
> demolished souls. Taxes . . . a new devaluation, a new set-
> tlement. Tension. They build a new settlement there; to-
> morrow, they'll build a new one here. Where shall I go
> then? To whom shall I protest?

Measures adopted against the residents—such as the denial of the right of political assembly, comprehensive censorship of the Arabic press, and periodic curfews over entire
towns and villages—have proved counterproductive, since
they cause increasing irritation and resentment among the
Palestinians. The efforts to build bridges between Israelis
and Palestinians have been dwarfed by actions which separate and antagonize them. One Israeli journalist commented: "It is now impossible to turn the wheel back and
begin a new framework of relations with the Palestinians
from the territories, because eleven years leave a bad
taste."[4] He quoted the words of a Palestinian friend: "We
are now moving toward future relations between us with a
bitter smile. . . . There are nice people among you, but we
hardly know them. We know the military governors, the soldiers who conduct searches, merchants from the big towns
in Israel, and the settlers and members of Gush Emunim."
The effectiveness of locally-initiated political action has
varied with the changes in the international diplomatic context. Thus, the teachers' strikes and student demonstrations in 1967 and 1968—which challenged the occupation,
the annexation of East Jerusalem, and the changes in the
educational and legal systems—were not supported by effective international pressure. The Arab régimes were still
stunned by their losses in 1967 and the Palestinian guerrilla
forces had not established diplomatic legitimacy. Those
early protests were silenced by arrests and deportations

that eliminated most of the prewar political élite and made most residents feel that political action was futile.

In contrast, the civil disobedience that began in 1975–76 helped to call attention to the occupation at a time when the Arab states had regained some diplomatic and military leverage and when the world community was more responsive to the political claims of the Palestinian people. Protests are still met by arrests and deportations, but international concern is more widespread and more sustained than in the late 1960's. Moreover, individuals and political groups have emerged within Israel who protest against infringements on educational institutions and against the establishment of Israeli settlements, and who believe that Israelis should live alongside—not dominate—Palestinians.

Over the past thirteen years, the political aims of the Palestinians on the West Bank and the Gaza Strip have altered substantially. These changes have been in response to changes in the international climate and have reflected the growth and maturation of nationalist sentiment. Immediately after the June War, Palestinian politicians of almost all parties called for a return to the *status quo ante*, since that seemed to be the one outcome that could win international support. From 1968 to 1970, the PLO gained popular support through its guerrilla warfare and revolutionary propaganda. It helped to reëstablish a sense of Palestinian political identity, but failed to establish a serious military presence. The ensuing period of diplomatic immobility, from 1970 to 1973, was reflected in the occupied territories by political paralysis and the expression of diverse political aims. Some sought to return to Jordan, either under the monarchy or under a reformed régime. Others adhered to the PLO demand for a state in all of Palestine. And some sought an independent state on the West Bank and Gaza. Given the widespread animosity toward King Hussein, the idea of a separate entity attracted considerable interest. However, most political figures believed that the Palestinians living under occupation lacked the power to end Israeli rule and achieve independence. Only after the PLO began to revise its strategy and support the idea of political activity specifically geared to the occupied territories did the politicians begin to seek a common national framework and unify their program.

The October War in 1973, which was initiated by the Egyptian and Syrian governments rather than the PLO or Jordan, proved to be a turning point in the Palestinian struggle. Nationalist fervor swept across the occupied territories. For the first time, Arab states had shown a credible military strength and considerable diplomatic skill, and so release from Israeli rule seemed imaginable. The nationalist politicians then adopted a dual strategy, both supporting the PLO as their representative and urging the PLO to concentrate on freeing the occupied territories from Israeli control. Support for the PLO was not coerced; rather, expressing such support was risky, since the military government might arrest political activists. In contrast, support for Jordan—which had been based on practical considerations rather than any popular appeal or legitimacy—reached its nadir. Furthermore, in the fall of 1974, when the Arab states endorsed the PLO as the Palestinians' representative, Jordan lost its official standing on the West Bank.

The nationalist drive was also fueled by reactions to Israeli measures, such as land expropriations and settlement bids, and sometimes reflected religious tension in Jerusalem and Hebron. The popular movement was not well organized, and therefore had an episodic character. The first opportunity to institutionalize the nationalist resurgence occurred in 1976, when municipal council elections enabled outspoken supporters of the PLO to attain public posts. But this local success was dissipated by external setbacks, notably the civil war in Lebanon and the diplomatic crisis over Sadat's initiative and the Camp David negotiations. The Palestinians living under occupation were disturbed by the polarization in the Arab world, hesitant about the Jordan-PLO rapprochement, and bitter at the policies of Menachem Begin's government.

The "autonomy" negotiations focused on the future of the West Bank and Gaza, but did not offer a genuine opportunity for Palestinian participation, unless the residents of the territories were willing to cut themselves off from the majority of Palestinians living outside. Although their fear of accepting autonomy arose in part from the opposition of both Jordan and the PLO to autonomy, the residents cannot be considered puppets of either Jordan or the PLO. There is constant political debate and ferment, questioning of Jordanian intentions and criticism of PLO policies. Nevertheless, politicians recognize the need for practical links with neighboring Jordan and view the PLO as both the institutional expression of the nationalist movement and their representative in the diplomatic arena. Although they press the PLO leadership to modify or change certain policies, they would not split from it and they comprehend the limitations on its freedom of action and the complicated cross-currents in which it operates.

Political Options

Even though the Palestinians reject the concept of autonomy when defined as self-rule under Israeli ultimate control, they do support negotiations to achieve an independent state alongside Israel. Moreover, they recognize that there should be a transition period prior to independence. During such a transition, the Palestinian ruling council would need to control basic resources such as land and water, wield financial authority, and handle administrative departments. The Palestinians on the West Bank and Gaza would require formal and informal links with the majority of fellow countrymen who live outside. These would include commercial links with Jordan, political ties with the PLO, and the right, in principle, for Palestinians to immigrate to the embryonic state.

At present (March 1980), the prospects for success in the autonomy negotiations appear dim, despite President Carter's invitation to Begin and Sadat to meet with him separately in Washington, D.C., in April 1980. If the negotiations follow their current course—with the Israeli government seeking to retain maximum control, accelerating the construction of settlements, and continuing to restrict political activity among the Palestinians, and the American and Egyptian governments registering only verbal protests— then a Palestinian boycott of elections for a "self-governing authority" is virtually assured. The authority would lack real power and would not be able to stop the absorption of the territories into Israel by the end of the transition period. In fact, accepting such an autonomy plan could jeopardize future Palestinian claims to self-determination and independence.

If, however, the autonomy negotiations result in the creation of a self governing authority that controls land and water resources, includes Jerusalem residents as voters and participants, and contains provisions to achieve full independence in the future alongside Israel, then the residents may face difficult choices. One can envisage three options emerging.

In the first option, if the US government has not established official contact with the PLO and has not improved its relations with Jordan, then the PLO and Jordan are certain to oppose the self-governing authority. In that event, residents of the West Bank and Gaza would boycott the elections, fearing total isolation in the Arab world and fearing that the potential for independence inherent in the accord would never be realized.

In the second option, Jordan might support self-rule but the PLO would oppose participation. That would seriously divide the Palestinians and invite coercion and retaliation from both Jordan and the PLO. Residents of the West Bank and Gaza view that situation as potentially the most dangerous, an outcome which most politicians have tried hard to prevent.

A third option would emerge if self-rule were attained in tandem with a broader set of discussions and negotiations, including an official US dialogue with the PLO and Jordan, and the opportunity for both to help set the terms of a transition period. Then the PLO and Jordan might support participation in the transitional self-governing authority, and the residents of the West Bank and Gaza would feel encouraged to stand for election. They would see a real possibility that the transition period could help them strengthen their social and economic institutions, create viable political structures, and absorb a significant number of refugees. In a relatively short period, an independent state could be created in such a way that it would meet the basic needs of the Palestinian people and would not threaten the security of Israel. Such an outcome is sought by responsible political leaders among the Palestinians, but statehood remains an elusive goal.

NOTES, CHAPTER 6

1. On economic aspects of the occupation, see Brian Van Arkadie, *Benefits and Burdens: A Report on the West Bank and Gaza Strip Economies since 1967* (New York: Carnegie Endowment for International Peace, 1977); review of Van Arkadie's book by Salim Tamari, *Gazelle Review*, number 3 (1978), pp. 115–8; Vivian Bull, *The West Bank—Is it Viable?* (Lexington, Mass.: Lexington Books, 1975); Elias H. Tuma and Haim Darin-Drabkin, *The Economic Case for Palestine* (London: Croom Helm, 1978); testimony by Salim Tamari and Ibrahim Dakkak, *The Colonization of the West Bank Territories by Israel*, October 18, 1977, U.S. Senate, Subcommittee on Immigration and Naturalization, Committee

on the Judiciary; Sheila Ryan, "The West Bank and Gaza," *MERIP Reports*, no. 74, January 1979, pp. 3–8; and Sarah Graham-Brown, "The West Bank and Gaza: The Structural Impact of Israeli Colonization," *MERIP Reports*, no. 74, January 1979, pp. 9–20.

2. Testimony by myself and Paul Quiring, *Israeli Settlements in the Occupied Territories*, hearings before the Subcommittees on International Organizations and on Europe and the Middle East, Committee on International Relations, House of Representatives, September 12, 1977, pp. 7–49; my articles on Israeli settlements in the *Journal of Palestine Studies*, no. 25, autumn 1977, pp. 26–47, and no. 29, autumn 1978, pp. 100–19; and Sarah Graham-Brown, "Water—How Israeli Politics Hurt West Bank Arabs," *Arab Report and Record* (London), May 23, 1979, pp. 4–6.

3. Excerpt from a paper delivered at a seminar, International Writers Program, Iowa City, Iowa, November 29, 1978.

4. Yehuda Litani, *Ha'aretz*, October 29, 1978.

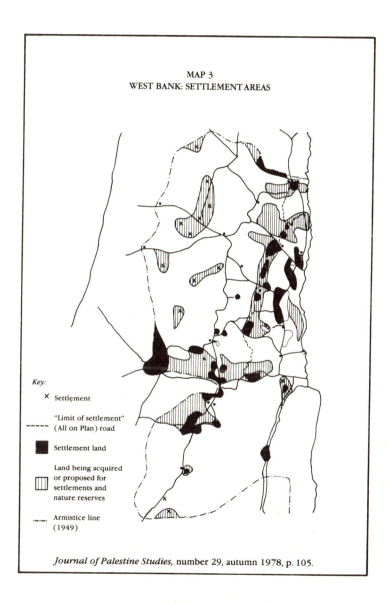

MAP 3
WEST BANK: SETTLEMENT AREAS

Key:

✕   Settlement

- - - -   "Limit of settlement" (All on Plan) road

■   Settlement land

▥   Land being acquired or proposed for settlements and nature reserves

-·-·-   Armistice line (1949)

Journal of Palestine Studies, number 29, autumn 1978, p. 105.

ABOUT THE AUTHOR

Dr. Ann Mosely Lesch served as the associate Middle East representative of the American Friends Service Committee, based in Jerusalem, from 1974 to 1977. Her academic research has focused on the history and contemporary issues surrounding the Israel-Palestine conflict. Her publications include *Arab Politics in Palestine, 1917–1939: The Frustration of a Nationalist Movement* (Ithaca, N.Y.: Cornell University Press, 1979); *The Politics of Palestinian Nationalism*, co-author with William B. Quandt and Fuad Jabber (Berkeley, Calif.: University of California Press, 1973); and *Israel's Occupation of the West Bank: The First Two Years* (Santa Monica, Calif.: The RAND Corporation, 1970).